THE CHAMBER MUSIC OF BRAHMS

BRAHMS IN 1895

From a photograph by Maria Fellinger

THE CHAMBER MUSIC OF

Brahms

BY

DANIEL GREGORY MASON

BOOKS FOR LIBRARIES PRESS
FREEPORT, NEW YORK

First Published 1933
Reprinted 1970

STANDARD BOOK NUMBER:
8369-5209-X

LIBRARY OF CONGRESS CATALOG CARD NUMBER:
78-107817

PRINTED IN THE UNITED STATES OF AMERICA

TO

GUSTAV OBERLAENDER

IS DEDICATED THIS BOOK,

made possible through the OBERLAENDER TRUST,
endowed by him to develop friendly understanding between America and the
German culture of which Brahms
is so fine a flower.

PREFACE

In offering to the public this book, the first, so far as I know, to be devoted entirely to the analytical study of all Brahms's chamber music works, I wish to acknowledge my obligation to the Oberlaender Trust, of the Carl Schurz Memorial Foundation, for making it possible for me to undertake the writing of it. I owe much not merely to Mr. Gustav Oberlaender, the generous founder of the Trust, but also to Dr. Wilbur K. Thomas, its Secretary, for many courtesies and kindnesses.

To the *Gesellschaft der Musikfreunde* in Vienna, where I spent some time studying the Brahms manuscripts, and especially to its Custodians Dr. Karl Geiringer and Dr. Hedwig Kraus, and to its Secretary Dr. Victor Luithlen, whose tireless assistance greatly aided me, I extend my cordial thanks, both for their forwarding of my work and for permission to enrich my book with the three facsimiles from manuscripts of Brahms chamber music works here reproduced for the first time.

In the possession of the *Gesellschaft der Musikfreunde* are the following manuscripts of Brahms: the String Quartets in C minor and in A minor, Opus 51; the last movement of the Piano Quartet in C minor, Opus 60; the Cello Sonata in F, Opus 99; the Trio in C minor, Opus 101; The Viola Quintet in G, Opus 111; and the Clarinet Quintet.

The manuscript of the G major Violin Sonata, Opus 78, is at the *Brahms Haus* in Gmunden, a museum founded by Brahms's friend Miller zu Aichholz on his property above the Traunsee.

Dr. Robert Fellinger of Berlin I thank for his kindness in providing me with the rather unusual frontispiece portrait, from a snapshot taken by his mother, Maria Fellinger, in the garden of her house in Vienna in October, 1895. Other portraits by the same hand, some of them more familiar in America than this one, the reader may see in *Brahms-Bilder*, von Maria Fellinger, Leipzig, Breitkopf und Härtel, 1911.

All the chamber music works except the seven duet sonatas (three for violin, two for violoncello, and two for clarinet) are obtainable in the excellently edited miniature scores of the Eulenberg Edition. The sonatas are published in the Simrock Edition. Brahms himself arranged as piano duets (for one piano, four hands) the two Sextets, the Piano Quartets in G minor and A major (but not the C minor), all three String Quartets, and the two Viola Quintets. The Piano Quintet he published also as a Sonata for Two Pianos, opus 34, b. The Clarinet Sonatas he issued for violin and piano as well as for viola and piano. Other of the chamber music works have been arranged, both for one piano, four hands and for two pianos, four hands—most of them published by Simrock. Even for piano solo Paul Klengel has made a few highly effective transcriptions, notably the Horn Trio, the two Viola Quintets, and the Clarinet Quintet.

It is hardly necessary to attempt here a complete bibliography. The standard life is Max Kalbeck's *Johannes Brahms*, eight volumes, *Deutsche Brahms-Gesellschaft*, Berlin, 1904–14. Florence May's *Life of Johannes Brahms* in two volumes, London, 1905, is useful for reference though critically unbalanced. Niemann's *Brahms* contains in the English translation (New York, 1929) a good bibliography. A thematic catalogue of the works is issued by Simrock, and the *Gesellschaft der Musikfreunde* has recently issued through Breitkopf und Härtel an edition of the Complete Works themselves, in twenty-six volumes. Studies in English are J. A. Fuller-Maitland, *Brahms*, London, 1911 (admirable in its criticism), W. H. Hadow, *Studies in Modern Music*, Second Series, London, 1895, and Daniel Gregory Mason, *From Grieg to Brahms*, new and enlarged edition, New York, 1927. Invaluable is Donald Francis Tovey's article in Cobbett's *Cyclopedic Survey of Chamber Music*, two volumes, London, 1929.

Several chapters of this book have appeared in various periodicals; and acknowledgement of permission to reprint is hereby made to the Editors of the Musical Times, London, of Musical America and the Musical Courier, New York, and of Disques, Philadelphia.

My friend Mr. Adolfo Betti, of the Flonzaley Quartet, has been so kind as to read in manuscript the chapters on the string quartets, and to make for them some interesting suggestions.

Finally, I venture to hope that this volume may prove useful not only to music-lovers wishing to understand the chamber music of Brahms, but to students of music in general, and particularly to composers. Brahms's technical skill and imaginative logic are so extraordinary, his grasp is so firm on all the elements of style, and especially on rhythm—so fundamental to musical plastic, and so comparatively neglected in our day—that the study of his works can hardly fail to prove highly liberating and stimulating to all open minds.

D. G. M.

New York,
January, 1933.

CONTENTS

xii   *Contents*

ILLUSTRATIONS

I

YOUTH

CHAPTER I

THE TRIO IN B MAJOR, OPUS 8

It is one of the ironies of music history that the first work in Brahms's great series of twenty-four masterpieces of chamber music—the Trio in B major, opus 8—should have come to its first performance, not in his native land, not even in Europe, but in our own then musically benighted America. The date was Tuesday, November 27, 1855. The place was Dodsworth's Hall, New York, on Broadway, opposite Eleventh Street and one door above Grace Church. The players were Theodore Thomas, violin, then only twenty years old, Carl Bergmann, cello, and William Mason, piano, a young man of twenty-six. The program, recorded in Dr. Mason's "Memories of a Musical Life", closed with the Brahms Trio, announced as "Grand Trio in B major, opus 8" (trios were always "grand" in those days). Dr. Mason's understatement that the piece was then played "for the first time in America" is misleading; it should read, "for the first time in the world". Florence May, in her "Life of Johannes Brahms", states specifically: "The Trio was performed for the first time in public, to the lasting musical distinction of America, on November 27, 1855, at William Mason's concert of chamber music in Dodsworth's Hall, New York. . . . It was played for the second time at Breslau on December 18 of the same year". If we compare this with the statement of Kalbeck that "The very first public performance . . . took place on December 18, 1855 in a chamber music soirée of Messrs. Machtig and Seyfriz in Breslau" it seems clear that Kalbeck has

3

fallen into error through not having heard of the New York performance, the priority of which is established by the dates.

As is well known, the Trio that Mason and his associates played on that Tuesday evening in November, 1855, written only a year before by the twenty-one-year-old composer (Brahms was born in Hamburg, May 7, 1833) was vastly different from the version we know today, revised by the mature master thirty-seven years later, in 1891, near the very end of his long life. There is hardly any analogue in all music history for this revision by a great master, in the heyday of his powers, of his very first chamber music work, exuberant with youthful genius, but also crude, turgid, and revealing on every page inexperience and bewilderment in face of problems that later became child's play to him. The confrontation of the two versions is thus of absorbing interest. We could ask for no better object lesson than they give, by their contrasts and possibly quite as much by their similarities, in precisely what constitutes Brahms's greatness.

The main themes of all four movements, to begin with, remain essentially unchanged: and great themes they are, sturdily moving along the diatonic scale in strongly articulated rhythms, recalling the simplicities of German folk-song that Brahms so dearly loved and so minutely studied. Take for instance the opening theme of the first movement, soaring and full of youthful ardor in each phrase, broadly and widely constructed as a whole with true Brahmsian "long breath". In William Mason's copy of the early version, still in existence, though the paper is flaking off at the edges and yellow with age,[1] the opening sixty-two measures are virtually identical with the same measures as they are shown in the Eulenberg miniature score of the later version.

---

[1] The early version is issued in a modern edition, convenient for study, by the Edition Breitkopf (No. 6051, "Erste Fassung").

Virtually, but not literally: Brahms at twenty-one, as at fifty-eight, started off his melody with the piano, continued it with the cello, and did not entrust it to the violin until the twenty-first measure. But the youthful Brahms was modest and timid, hospitable like all really good craftsmen to suggestions; and he had a friend, the great violinist Joseph Joachim, whom at that time he regarded as his superior in composition, and who all his life continued to exercise a profound influence upon him. So in deference to the wishes of his friend, who did not like the violin to be kept so long silent, he introduced for it some insignificant and otiose little scraps of counterpoint against the cello melody, to be seen to this day in the old edition, but stricken out when he grew old enough to know what he really did not want.

But our interest in the first theme, far deeper than one in superficial detail, goes right to the root of structural relationships that must be understood by anyone who wishes to understand its composer's work as a whole. To put the case bluntly, we may say that the young Brahms's theme (No. I in Figure 1), ironically enough by its best qualities—its firm pace, strong lyric individuality, and noble proportions, defeats his immature skill when he seeks to fit it as a part into a complete sonata movement.

The theme owes its dignity to a number of noteworthy peculiarities. First of all, it is not a short pregnant fragment, such as Beethoven likes to use as a main theme, but a complete lyric melody, laid out on a scale truly Schubertian in its deliberation. The mere bulk of the theme might not have raised an insoluble problem had not two other features of it presented pitfalls. First, like so many of Brahms's melodies, it is very rugged and simple in its harmonic basis: like the German folksongs he so loved, it grows out of the fundamental tonic and dominant harmonies, and follows the line of the diatonic

scale. This is admirable; but unless the other themes afford
contrast, it is a pitfall. Secondly, and more seriously still, its

rhythmic movement is strongly "thetic"—placing the important notes solidly on the accented beats: if we count its half-
note beats aloud, emphasizing the important notes, it reads thus:

> "*One*, two, *One*, two
> *One*, two, *One*, two" etc.

The scene is set, then, for the discomfiture of the youthful
composer. We can follow the stages of it with an amusement
not unmixed with pity.

His first misstep, fatal, irremediable, is the adoption of a
second and a third theme (II and III, in Figure 1) which do
nothing to afford contrast to the thetic rhythm of the first, but

turn its weightiness to downright heaviness by their pitiless insistence on beat One. To make bad worse, Brahms associates
with his second theme a fugue subject, reserved for extended use
later, of the most conventional "school" type, again relentlessly
insistent on beat One. The result is that, having no essential
rhythmic contrast to help him, he finds his second theme un-
accountably wearisome, especially in the breadth of proportions
the scale of the main theme imposes upon him, and in the hope
of relieving this monotony speeds up his fundamental pace. He
has now broken his sonata-form into fragments as unmendable
as those of the fallen Humpty Dumpty. Anyone who will play
through themes II and III at a natural pace, and then try to
go on, *at the same pace,* with theme I, will see that this false
remedy for monotony of rhythm has both left it uncured, and
introduced essential lack of unity into the whole movement.
(Theme I cannot, in fact, be resumed after II and III without
change of pace,—a cruel psychological *donnée* which involves
Brahms, at the beginning of the repetition of his themes, in a
fruitless effort to bridge back:—Brahms, later to become the
supreme modern master of rhythm!)

The clue to the success of the later version is the second
theme which, as brief and to the point as its complex nature
will permit, takes in it the place of the earlier prolix and
monotonous second theme, fugue subject, and third theme.
This new and beautiful theme is shown at Figure 2, a. The
clue again to the effectiveness of this theme, one of the
finest in all Brahms, is its real contrast with the first, both by
the elusive chromatic steps which its melody opposes to the
diatonic vigor of the other, and more especially by its masterly
combination of metrical conformity to the first with profound
and essential rhythmic contrast to it. This theme is not thetic,
but anacrustic: that is to say, its note-groups begin not on the
beats but before the beats. If we follow the common custom of

calling a half-beat "And," we shall find that it must be counted as follows:

"*And* One and two, *And* One and two
And one *and* two *and One* . . . two."

figure 2.

In the eight measures of retransition to the repeat of his themes Brahms not only avoids the laughable gaucheries of the first version but introduces a triplet figure of subordinate rhythm that kills at least five birds with one stone:

1. It holds back the pace to a breadth that ends the exposition with great dignity.

2. It echoes with a difference the previous triplets of page 4, measure 3 (Eulenberg miniature score), thus serving the unity of the whole.

3. It prepares an interesting figure in the development (most of page 8).

4. It gives the figuration needed for the recapitulation of the main theme, as we shall see in more detail later.

5. It gives the cue for the slightly modified, completely charming, figure used in the coda (last four measures of page 17).

By thus reducing the three themes of his original version to two which embody a real contrast in a fundamental unity, Brahms has done more than turn a non-sequacious, messy exposition section into a highly cogent and stirring one; he has prepared the way for transforming his whole movement from its initial prolix incoherence into its final magnificent directness. To observe the change in all its fascinating detail must be left to individual students. We must be content here to examine briefly a few of the most salient results.

Take for instance the matter of the recapitulation of the themes, that stumbling block on which sonata-form so often wrecks the unwary. In the early version Brahms brings back his themes with all the helpless literalness, the equable insistence on the important and the unimportant alike, with which children tell stories. Contrast the subtle way in which, at the bottom of page 12 in the new version (Eulenberg) the main theme steals in in the strings, not in the original B major but in the related and as it were veiled key of G sharp minor, the piano meanwhile steadying the pace with the triplet figure already prepared. Note how it gradually acquires force, until at the bottom of the next page it asserts itself more strongly than ever—thanks largely to those same triplets. Above all, note how even this new force of statement is heightened by the incomparable force of brevity, sixty-two measures boiling down to twenty-one, or about a third of the original statement.

But the most striking contrast of all is that between the two codas. In the early version Brahms is hopelessly beaten before he starts by the facts, first, that he has nothing new to say about his central theme, and second, that his other two themes are too like it in rhythm to afford him any effective contrast. Hence, as proverbially is always the case with those who have nothing to say, he takes to ranting: his last two pages are devoted to *fortissimo* shoutings of the theme which, since their noise is quite unsupported by new thought, leave us unmoved, while the final cadence is mere Lisztian bombast oddly out of character in Brahms: a pompous succession of trite chords *"con tutta forza"*—in short, the false sublime. It all reminds us of the wind's effort, in the fable, to make the traveller take off his coat; and the more it blusters the more we turn up our coat collars in indifference, and go about our business.

It is only in the second version that the sun comes out. With the abatement of the pace to *Tranquillo,* cello and violin begin to alternate the phrases of the main theme, emphasizing in each fragment the suspension that forms its expressive essence, the violin soon turning it into sequences which prolong and intensify it. The piano too joins in, seeking the subdominant key that almost invariably lends its restfulness to Brahms's codas, and dying out *(perdendo)* through groups of three eighth-notes generated from the suspensions, to rhythmic obliteration and silence. Then, in the moment of profoundest tenderness quoted in Figure 2, b, as if reborn from these groups of three eighth-notes, the three quarter-notes of the second theme, their anacrustic attack restored, are distilled to a new concentration. Their downward form draws a new tension from its harmonization in seventh-chords, their upward form is given the touching simplicity of unison utterance, first by the violin and then by the cello; and when the piano takes it in both directions at once, that subdominant seventh chord with raised fourth step that Brahms so dearly loves, and the wide spread in register, touch it to a real exaltation. Finally some quicker, more energetic forms of the same suspensions lead to a vigorous conclusion.

For the sake of our good understanding of later examples, it will be worth while to record here the general points this beautiful coda illustrates.

1. Isolation of the most essential part of the main theme, and multiplication of it by sequence, with heightening of its most significant features—in this case the suspension.

2. Use of subdominant key to give sense of repose.

3. Brief reference, also expressively heightened, to a contrasting theme.

4. To restore vigor of emotional tone after these poignancies, a short passage in more rapid movement (a sort of "sprint") to the end.

Of the other movements the scherzo, with its staccato playfulness and mystery and the broad-gauged enthusiasm of its trio, undergoes little change. The finale profits by a new, a more vigorous and direct, second theme. The *Adagio*, naturally of all four movements the profoundest in expression, affords striking evidence of the essential unity of its composer's musical character throughout his life. For the noble poising song of the cello, punctuated by pondering questions from the piano, which he added in 1891 (Figure 3, b and c), provides the exact completion our feeling demands for the hollow, mystical harmonies of the opening theme, conceived by the youth of twenty-one (Figure 3, a). That needed a companion that could bring its almost celestial beauty down to earth, and into men's questioning

Figure 3.

hearts; and this was what he gave it in the rewriting, and what turned the finished slow movement from a torso of high promise into the first of those incomparable poems that are the great slow movements of his best chamber music works.

CHAPTER II

THE SEXTET IN B FLAT, OPUS 18

THE peculiar psychological interest, among all Brahms's works in chamber music, of the first Sextet, composed in his late twenties, is that in it we see him definitely taking the step from childhood to manhood: a step difficult for all, by many never taken, so fully achieved as he finally achieved it by very few. The Sextet marks unmistakably the moment of his musical adolescence. In the Trio, opus 8 he had thrown himself, with all the exuberance of youth, into romanticism, with its narrow subjectivity, its wilfulness, its restless search for novelty of material, its turgidity and incoherence. And he had been acclaimed by the arch-romantic, Schumann, in the historic article "New Paths."

Then came a dramatic pause. What, after all, were these new paths to be? Should he go on, in the same impulsive, undisciplined way, pouring out his personal feelings and fancies, with no attempt to give them any larger, more objective beauty? Or should he set himself patiently to master that classic art of necessity which unfolds with the inevitability of the reason that inspires it? Given the nature of Brahms, modest, receptive, full of eager curiosity, impatient of mere personal idiosyncrasy, deeply craving universal beauty, there could be no question of the answer.[1]

Impersonal mastery could be achieved only through "play-

[1] See the present writer's *From Grieg to Brahms,* pages 181-185; also *Artistic Ideals,* the chapter on "Originality."

ing the sedulous ape" to the great models. In the Sextet it is easy to recognize influences. Its scherzo shouts at us "Beethoven," and even "Seventh Symphony." Its finale is made on a rondo theme that might well have been signed "Haydn" or "Mozart." And the lilting A major theme in the first movement, an Austrian ländler or slow waltz to the life, irresistibly suggests the equally Viennese Schubert. But the change in point of view is more striking than the influences it makes room for. A maturing of personality has taken place which makes the composer imaginatively aware of other minds and hearts, so that he instinctively rejects mere secretion of mood in favor of communication of feeling.

Method naturally changes commensurately. It is only necessary to assemble the themes of the opening movement (see Figure 4) to realize that while pace unifies them as it failed to unify those of the Trio, each has its own strongly marked rhythm, by which in any environment it is individualized. Theme I, like the themes of the Trio, is "thetic": its strong notes, that is to say, come on the theses, or accented beats. The "ländler" theme is also thetic, but in a subtly contrasting way: the measures being alternately strong and weak, the heaviest notes—the dotted halves—come not where we should expect them, in the heavy measures, but in the light measures, while the light notes come in heavy measures. (It is well known that the placing of light or quick notes on a heavy measure or beat—as in so many Beethoven scherzos—gives the feeling of gaiety and humor so charming here.) Theme II begins with an anacrusis (on the third or "up" beat) and is notably graceful throughout. Theme III presents a favorite rhythmic device of Brahms. As its first note belongs to what has gone before, it begins virtually with an "empty first beat," so that its whole progress up to the high F, and later to the high A, somewhat resembles a prolonged anacrusis—a breathless, forward-straining effect that gives it a fine momentum. Thus the four themes present the variety of fundamental rhythm essential to a well-coördinated movement.

Figure 4.

This leads us to a still more subtle problem of construction. In the early Trio the young Brahms fails not only to invent contrasting rhythms for his themes but also to build the uniform themes into an intelligibly unfolding, dramatically convincing fabric. In the development section especially, the themes seem to enter unexpectedly, as it were arbitrarily, and to disappear without clinching any definite impression; they give, in short, an effect both of monotony and of miscellaneity. Here, on the other hand, with far more various themes, the transitions are so flowing that we pass easily back and forth, and our final impression is no less satisfying for its unity than for its variety. How has this surprising improvement been attained?

If we look more closely at the Eulenberg score, we shall see that each new rhythm is carefully "prepared," as the playwrights say, before it actually appears. For instance, the rhythm of Theme II, which does not actually enter in the first cello until the bottom of page 7, is prepared as early as the last measure of page 4 (first violin part); the ländler is prepared a page before it enters, in the cadence at page 5, measures 10–11; and Theme III, destined to appear in the fifth measure of page 9, is prepared not only very deliberately in the four measures immediately preceding it, but more casually in the cadence of the first cello announcing Theme II. If we analyze the psychological effect upon us of these preparations we shall see that they contribute immensely to the intelligibility of the whole piece: they show us what to expect, and yet by remaining only fragments of it make it all the more satisfying when it arrives in its entirety. One peculiarity of their usual location is worth mentioning: they are apt to fall, as in three of the four cases just cited, within the cadences. The reason is that while clearness usually compels the composer to devote the beginnings of his phrases to the themes then holding the stage, their endings or cadences are available for "plants"— to borrow another term from the dramatists—of themes presently to come. In later works Brahms becomes extraordinarily skilful in thus deftly insinuating in the conclusion of one theme a suggestion of what the next theme is to be and so carrying us along with him sociably, as befits a mature mind, in the un-foldment of his fabric, instead of plunging us arbitrarily into new phases with childish impulsiveness.

The technical means by which one prepares are modified repetitions. It is surprising how much of the technique of classically objective music can be best understood as modified repetition, either on a small or a large scale, affecting, that is to say, either the molecules or the larger masses of the music. Yet perhaps it is not so surprising either, if we reflect that music, un-rolling itself before us in time, can become intelligible only through repetitions (comparable to the balances and symmetries of visual art), and that these repetitions are naturally given in-terest chiefly by minor modifications, at once stimulating and satisfying our curiosity.

This may be seen in the molecular structure of all the themes cited from the Sextet. In I, note how measures 4–5 repeat 2–3, with the significant alteration of the high F, made more prominent by being pulled forward to the third beat. The repetitions by two-measure sections in the ländler are almost obvious, but in the continuation on page 7 of the score the modification of F sharp, heard twice, to an F natural the third time, is a happy instance of this kind of musical fancy. In Themes II and III the play with identical rhythmic figures in different parts is of the highest fascination. Glancing at the other movements, it will be evident how largely the scherzo is created out of such playfulness. The theme of the variations, in the *Andante*, a nobly rugged tune, makes use of the same principle in a different way. Here the modifications derive their interest from the placing of incompatible notes close together; the C of measure 6 with the C sharp of measure 8; the C of measure 2 in the second half with the C sharp of measure 4; and the F sharps of measures 5 and 6, making room just in time for the F naturals of the

Part I.   Figure 5.

Andante, ma moderato.

This part is repeated, in fuller sonority

Part II.

Part II also repeated in fuller sonority

last two measures! It is worth while to go through the whole movement, noting how much of its interest derives from this witty confrontation of irreconcilables.

"Variations"—the very word sums up the idea of modified repetition. And it is by no means a matter of chance that Brahms, in whose mature work the ideal of interest of detail on a basis of simple and therefore universally intelligible idiom entirely displaces his early fondness for superficially novel effects, was as fond of variation-writing as Bach and Beethoven. In his twenty-four chamber music works he devotes six movements specifically to this delightfully intellectual form: the slow movements of both Sextets, the finale of the B flat Quartet, the slow movement of the Trio, opus 87, the finale of the Clarinet Quintet, and the finale of the E flat Clarinet Sonata. Moreover, in all his works of the middle and later periods the variation, whether avowed or not, is constantly present as a principle.

Even in so early a work as the Sextet, the most interesting variation is not in the Variations at all, but in the finale; and it is varied, as so often happens with the most thoughtful composers, not by complication but by simplification. Here is the theme of the finale, a jolly tune in the vein of Haydn, and, underneath it, the dialogue Brahms draws from it. (See Figure 6.) The instruments alternate in the chord pairs, the violins and first viola for the high ones, the second viola and the cellos for the low ones, so that the ear is charmed by the contrasts of color enhancing the essential idea of give and take. But as the passage demands the assistance of our imagination, since what was first presented as a coherent melody must now be picked up from detached blocks providing its underlying harmonies, it is chiefly the mental ear that is delighted. The simplifying variation always has this supreme merit of rousing our imaginations. Only by their active aid can it be understood.

The principle of modified repetition is here no less pervasively at work in the larger masses of the music, notably the development of the first movement, than in its molecular tissue. In this development the ideas are not taken up and dropped again almost at random, as were those of the Trio, but laid out deliberately in three sections, each with a function to perform in building up dramatic effect. The first is elaborated from the main theme, and extends through three pages, the anacrustic rhythms on page 11 and the increasing sonority and rhythmic agitation of pages 12 and 13 making it constantly

Figure 6.

more exciting. The second is a charming lull, on the ländler theme, in the remote and cool key of E minor. The third, beginning at the middle of page 15, is the most masterly of all. It is a subtly planned "preparation," on the first three notes of the main theme, so mysterious in their tentative harmonization and their low position on the cello that we hardly recognize them until the theme triumphantly breaks forth in the three middle instruments, *forte,* and in the original key . . . As simply and broadly planned as the development is also the irresistible coda, with its tender Goodbye to the chief theme and its coy *pizzicato* play with Theme III at the very end.

The B flat Sextet is far from being as personal to Brahms as some of his later works; in the obviousness of its indebtedness to earlier masters it is even perhaps inferior in a certain narrow kind of originality to the B major Trio. But it is the first piece of chamber music in which, freeing himself once for all from the subjectivity and turgidity of romanticism, he starts to explore the road of classic universality in beauty, in which he was to discover such unprecedented treasures.

CHAPTER III

THE PIANO QUARTET IN G MINOR, OPUS 25

In January, 1863, a few months before he turned thirty, Brahms took one of the decisive steps of his life in leaving his native Hamburg, where he had passed not only his youth but some of the important years of intensive study that followed his acclaim by Schumann, and in turning for his permanent headquarters to Austria, to that gaiety and artistic sensitiveness of the Austrians to which strong ties already bound him. For the rest of his life, he owed as much to Vienna, and gave it in return as much of the divining interpretation of his genius, as did his great predecessors Haydn, Mozart, Beethoven, and Schubert.

In the youthful works written in the Detmold and Hamburg periods of his late twenties—the B flat Sextet, the G minor and A major Quartets with piano, and the great F minor Piano Quintet in which their special vein of style culminated,—we see already the essential qualities of his early Viennese period. It is significant that though in Vienna fame came to him quickly, he was accepted there at first more as pianist than as composer. And in the Quartets and the Quintet he is obviously putting his best foot forward as a pianist, writing more from the standpoint of the virtuoso, less from that of the poet and thinker, than he ever did again. Secondly, the folk elements in his style, both the German folk-song vein with its tonic-dominant harmonies and its melodious thirds and sixths that almost bring before our eyes the groups of singers on a Rhine boat,

and the more specifically Hungarian and even gipsy elements
that familiarity with Austrian life had long endeared to him,
now begin to color strongly his personal style, though still
curiously mingled with less congenial elements later extruded.
Finally there is in these works the fecundity of idea, verging
sometimes on prolixity if not even on loquacity, appropriate

Figure 7.

to impetuous youth. The melodies tumble over one another's
heels, spring out of each other as they run. Indefatigable renewal of energy, amplitude of development, luxuriance of
thought, are at the pole from the master's later laconism. This
is still the music of youth, though the youth be that of a Titan.

The amount of elbow-room needed by the youthful Brahms
in a sonata-form allegro is strikingly illustrated by that of the
G minor Quartet. Everything is here on large scale. Each
section is composed of two or more contrasting ideas, and

joined to its neighbor by an amply conceived transition. The exposition alone fills nine and a half pages of the Eulenberg miniature score. First comes the main theme, divided in Mozartean fashion into two contrasting parts, a pregnant melodic pattern of four notes (Figure 7, a) and a tender bit of melody

Figure 8.

(7, b) in folk-songish thirds and sixths. Considerable development of these leads over to a broadly lyric melody in D Minor that we at first take to be the second theme, but that proves to be only a sort of under-study and transition to it ("Bridge"). II itself, when it does come, is in D major, and scored with almost orchestral richness, only suggested in shorthand in the illustration. (See Figure 8.) This in turn carries us to the first part of the conclusion theme (III), thirds and sixths again, with a drone bass like a bagpipe and a truly peasant-like boisterousness of mood. We feel sure this is to end the exposition; but the stream of melody is too rich and full not to form a final eddy or two: the delightful play with a subsidiary figure on page 10 of the score, and the farewell-taking to the principal four-note motive that occupies page 11. . . . The development is truly heroic in conception; and the recapitulation, though somewhat shortened from the exposition, and magically transformed, equals it in Jovian spaciousness. There is a long and richly fanciful coda.

If we were to judge such an example of sonata-form by an arbitrary standard based on, say, the first movement of Beethoven's Fifth Symphony, or even that of Brahms's own last chamber music work, the E flat Clarinet Sonata, we should have to say it was inexcusably diffuse. Yet as we listen to it we find there is not a dull moment, and not one that is irrelevant. How is such a miracle accomplished?

No doubt much credit must go to the skill of the piano writing, to the equal instinct for the treatment of the strings, and to the resulting purely sensuous magnificence of the *fortissimos* and loveliness of the *pianissimos*. Considering the constant variety and felicity of the sound, it is puzzling how the notion, "Brahms does not sound," ever got about. Probably the anecdotes of his roughness, the boldness of the *forte* passages, and perhaps a lingering memory of the Beckerath drawing of him sitting at the piano like a powerful if friendly bear, worked in people's minds to create the superstition of his "harshness" and "heaviness." Certainly there is a Promethean daring in his big moments: witness the *fortissimo* statement of the main theme, with its massed unisons of strings and its piano figures in sixteenth-notes going off like minute guns; or, in the slow movement, the military passage in C major; or, in the Rondo alla Zingarese, passage after passage worthy of the gipsies in their impetuous fire.

But there are other moments equally characteristic and, if not so stirring, even more beautiful, in which it is no longer the superhuman strength of this bear of music that impresses us, but his nose for honey. Such for instance are the opening of the recapitulation (Score, page 17) in sunniest G major, after the glooms and strenuosities of the development; the close of the delicious Intermezzo, and the whole of its delicate Trio and coda; and even the quieter moments in the almost rowdy Rondo that forms the finale. Above all, ponder the sea-change that overtakes the third theme of the first movement on its return at page 21 of the score. Formerly it was boisterous like a peasants' dance; now it whispers as sadly as leaves in autumn, whether from the strings or from the piano. One cannot too much admire the exact instinct for the style appropriate to the two media with which the composer here transforms his theme.

Far more subtle than the sensuous charm is the transformation of the thought itself. Deeply characteristic of Brahms is the constant renewal of the musical thought of which we have already seen an example in the prolongation of the bridge into the kindred but different second theme. His music is always in flux; and as it moves, it blossoms and flowers. Indeed, the intellectual and emotional grasp revealed in this unceasing reshaping of the musical thoughts, especially in their rhythmic coördination, is probably his fundamental quality.

In order to get a vivid impression of this, let us take a single musical idea, the four-note motive that opens the Quartet, and trace a few of its manifold transformations. We have already described the stormy vigor of the bold form it takes on page 4 of the score. Let us here rather choose a quieter, more imaginative moment—the reminiscence of it just at the close of the exposition. Note first that the troubled, mysterious character its original statement took from beginning on the dominant, and in minor mode, now (Figure 9) gives place to contentment and finality (centreing on the tonic; major mode). In the fifth measure an expansion of the jump leads to a

Figure 9

modulation into E flat, after which, by delightfully gradual falls, punctuated by the two notes only which now remain from the four of the motive, and which themselves, by a particularly beautiful touch, turn their direction at the ninth measure downward rather than upward, it sinks down to its centre of gravity on D.

In the development section, on the contrary, we have an irresistible gradual rise in intensity to highly dramatic turbulence, produced partly by tonal, far more by rhythmic evolution. Figure 10 shows but a few phases of it. At a, *pianis-*

simo, the left hand of the pianist begins, and is "imitated" after half a measure by the right: all is mysterious, in half-light. At b, *piano,* the strings imitate the piano after half a measure. The suspensive harmony makes this more exciting than a, but rhythmically both are still thetic, the figures beginning on accented beats. On comparing the effect of c, *mezzo forte,* we realize at once the immense force of rhythm: the anacrustic placing of the strings with their opening note on a weak beat moves the whole forward with relentless impetus. Finally, in the coda, by the simple device of tying the last note in each group to the first of the next, and dovetailing the instruments so that piano and strings move alternately, the composer builds his motive to *fortissimo,* and then allows it to fade away to nothing. (Figure 10, d.) In all these cases, no cleverness of detail could take the place of this quiet choice of the right pattern, which is then allowed to work out its inevitable course with the majesty of a process of nature.

It is curious that this young composer, already so complete a master of structure, is still feeling his way in the matter of style, and often oscillates uncertainly between melodic idioms properly his own and others borrowed from influential contemporaries. A feature of melody in fairly general use, for instance, in the middle of the nineteenth century, especially among operatic composers, is the "essential turn." In Wagner we find it prominent already in "Lohengrin" and "Tannhäuser," and persisting even into the period of "Tristan," where it reaches its apotheosis in the "Love-Death." To the soberer, more reserved style of Brahms, averse to ornateness, it is basically uncongenial, yet it permeates his early works like a childish habit still to be outgrown. We find it in the main themes of three out of the four movements of the B flat Sextet, and of two out of the four of the Quartet (the first and the slow movements). To the bridge and second themes of the first

Figure 10.

movement, as may be seen in Figure 8, it imparts an oddly Wagnerian flavor.

Similarly, the C major "Animato" section of the slow movement is full of operatic clichés. The broken triplets of its third and fourth measures have a Lisztian swagger, a pretentious pomposity utterly at variance with the Brahmsian candor; and they are even worse when on the next page they are imposed on melodramatically altered harmonies. All the cadences in this section are stale rubber-stamps of a banality surprising even in the youthful work of a composer who elsewhere shows himself such a master of cadence. He seems to be diverting himself, like a youth at a fancy-dress ball, by trying on all the costumes, swords, and wigs; and we never know when we are to see him "in his own features," and when behind some preposterous false nose. Thus the chief melody of the Andante, which begins in a vein worthy of Beethoven or mature Brahms for nobility (Figure 11, a) ends with a cadence (11, b) which for cheap sentimentality is probably not equalled elsewhere in its composer's complete works.

As the slow movement is on the whole the one in which uncertainty of style leads, despite fine moments, to the most pronounced incongruity, so, however likeable the verve of the gipsyish Rondo, and however splendid the intellectual mastery of the opening Allegro, of all four movements the most personal in style, the most inimitable in its elusive charm, is surely the Intermezzo. Here, for the first time in the chamber music works, we find a type of light movement destined to become as characteristic of Brahms as the scherzo of boisterous horseplay, or of fanciful mystery is of Beethoven, or that of fairy-like delicacy is of Mendelssohn. Brahms likes to smile rather than to laugh; his ever alert mind enjoys the play with humor as much as the shaping and interpretation of sentiment; and the type of movement he increasingly substitutes for the minuet or the scherzo of earlier masters is a gracefully fanciful intermezzo like this, tinged with wistfulness or even melancholy, and indulging to the full his taste for the phantasmagoria of shifting rhythms.

Now rhythmic contrasts are best gauged by our minds against some steady measuring figure to which they can be referred; and it is noticeable in how many movements of this type Brahms sets a regularly pulsing meter in some one part,

Figure 11.

as here in the cello. Although such a persistent pulse has something of the suppressed excitement of the drums of savages, its final effect is never with Brahms merely primitive, as it so often is for example with Tschaikowsky, because his real interest is centered not in the figure for itself, but in the subtle rhythms which by reference to it may be effectively opposed. In the present instance there are three themes, all differing in

rhythm: the opening pensive melody in sixths, with its characteristic downward anacruses; the piano theme in G major at
the bottom of the first page, accenting always the second of the
three beats; and the more sustained, almost lyric melody that
enters in the violin in F minor, and completes a lovely phrase
with Brahmsian groups of two notes against three. Throughout the intermezzo these contrasting rhythms relieve each
other, their interest heightened by modulations caused by
basses creeping up to unexpected points, and as it ends, the
combination of the first two, all through page 32, produces an
irresistible wavering of accent. There is a brittle, piquant trio.

We thus see, in the G minor Quartet, the composer struggling to form a personal style from the elements of German
and Hungarian folk-song, of gipsy music, and of the con-
tributions of Bach, Beethoven, Haydn, Mozart, Schubert, and
others that make up his musical heritage. For the moment his
success is only partial. Yet it holds good promise for the
future—a promise to be realized, much more unequivocally
than here, in the very next work, the Piano Quartet in A major,
opus 26.

CHAPTER IV

THE PIANO QUARTET IN A MAJOR, OPUS 26

FROM the point of view of depth of feeling and complete individuality of style the finest movements of the A major Quartet are surely the first two—as happens to be the case also with the G minor. Certain technical and stylistic points, however, illustrated by the last two movements (the scherzo and the finale), are so interesting in themselves and so enlightening as to the growth of the composer's mastery of his art, that we may well examine them first, coming back to the greater movements with an enlarged understanding.

The dryness of the scherzo on a first hearing inclines us to sympathize with the anti-Brahmsian who spoke of its "scrap-basket theme":—a theme, that is, in itself so uninteresting that its busy development comes near being a bore, and we almost wish it had found repose in the scrap-basket. Even its treatment somewhat emphasizes its shred-like nature. Yet what strikes us as we continue to study it is the consummate skill with which these shreds are woven into an eventually coherent texture, the contrapuntal mastery with which they are ordered. And we remember that in those days Brahms was constantly exchanging contrapuntal exercises with his friend Joachim, and that then and later he accepted no Schoenbergian misfits in his counterpoint, but insisted it must be smooth and clear as well as musically significant. . . . The trio is also contrapuntal, a canon on one of Brahms's gigantesque themes, in which strings answer piano after one measure. Not very persuasive or winning music is this, perhaps, the trio any more than the scherzo; but it is written with the skill of a young master.

As for the finale, the first thing we feel about it is that, in the expressive German phrase, it is *langweilich;* it shares to the full the diffuseness of the earlier Quartet in G minor. In rondo form, it lets us hear its folk-songish main theme no less than six times—the fourth time developed, the fifth rhythmically remodelled. Between the repetitions are transitions and contrast themes, in rather too generous measure. But this prolixity is not to be confused with the uncoördinated juxtaposition of the early version of the Opus 8 Trio, where the themes fall into incompatible tempi, and will not truly coalesce. Here on the contrary the coördination is perfect, even if the scale is large.

Meanwhile, noteworthy as the finale may be for its comparative prolixity, it is even more so for the light it throws on the formation of its composer's style, especially on the gradual emergence of some particularly personal traits. In the C major section, for instance, the half-note beats which in the lively main theme contained whole groups of quarters and eighths, with much vigorous syncopation, are taken as unbroken units of melody. In other words, while the steadiness of pulse necessary to the unity of a sonata movement is secured by the uniform value of the beats, the relation of these beats to the rhythm changes, the former groups giving place to single units referring to still larger groups, so that the rhythm becomes more stately. From Figure 12 we can learn a number of interesting things.

First of all, in this passage what Weingartner has called the "Brahms leit-motive," made from the tones of the common chord with one omitted, in such fashion as to produce a characteristic jump, emerges so strongly in the fourth measure (do

not count the opening half-measure), and is harped upon by
such quick reiteration in the next three, that no one could doubt
for a moment what one composer in the whole world wrote it.
The Wagnerian "essential turn" in the next to the last measure
here becomes entirely subordinate, while the leit-motive signs
"Brahms" to the passage as unequivocally as his own signature

Figure 12.

could do; and it is made all the more characteristic by the dovetailing with its imitation on the piano, below, and by the peculiar rhythmic hobbling that results.

The motive here arises, however, as only a detail in a
larger process to which the passage owes its real rationale.
What Brahms is doing, as befits so thoughtful a composer, is
meditating on a single tone, G, in the strings, answered by another single tone, C, in the piano. He jumps down to the G,
first from B, then from the higher E (accenting it, to make us
notice the widening interval), and finally from the octave G

itself, in the characteristic melody of the leit-motive and with the increasing agitation of more motion. It is as if he were *thinking aloud* about the musical significance of this G. And then finally, at the moment the piano takes it away from the violin, another much repeated tone, the B flat in the left hand, changes to A sharp, forcing the G to become the tonic of the new key of G, and so making it more important than ever. In this short passage, then, we are not only induced to put purely superficial ornaments like the essential turn in their place, but we are made to feel once for all that the primary concern of its composer is with the musical thought, with the profound significances that may attend the changing values of even single tones, provided they be illuminated by the steady glow of the musical imagination.

A good deal of the transcendent beauty of the first two movements of the Quartet is traceable to the deep expressiveness of this same manner of insisting on single tones. In the main theme of the *Poco Adagio* (Figure 13, a), one of the most sustained that even Brahms ever wrote, a peculiar and very lovely color is obtained by giving to the muted strings, represented in our illustration by the left hand part, slurred note-groups in each of which the same tone presently to be played in the piano melody is anticipated. All sorts of delicate clashes result, giving a peculiarly rich texture to the essentially simple music. What is undoubtedly the most striking single passage in the movement grows out of a different kind of insistence on a single tone. The first theme ends with the cello harping on low E in a strongly emotional figure (Score, bottom of page 22). As the piano smears, at first softly, then with increasing range and power, an arpeggio on the diminished seventh chord on E, cello alone, then cello and viola, finally cello, viola, and violin repeat the same figure in widening intervals and with increasing intensity until, carrying everything before it, it

Figure 13.

*This chord is arpeggiated as in Figure 14.

forces its way into a new key. A shorthand version of this
passage, in which the arpeggios may be represented by solid
chords, will suffice to show its imaginative power. (Figure
13, b). Finally, the main theme of the first movement also

builds itself out of a significant oscillation, first between C sharp
and A, then between C sharp and A sharp (Figure 13, c); but
here the melodic interest is intensified by some of Brahms's
favorite rhythmic devices: the omission of the accented note
(at the start of the second beat) and the group of three notes
to a beat contrasted with two to a beat.

Even more than in the materials, however, arresting as
these are, the composer's imagination displays its full glory
in their development. Here we become conscious of a new and
more mature quality, mingling with the garrulous youthful
romanticism and frequently displacing it:—a certain strictness
and sparseness, an insistence on the lowest terms, the most
laconic presentation of every idea, that begin to give the music
a new cleanness and austerity, a concentration as exciting as that
of mathematics. If it be true that the greatest music and the
greatest mathematics are alike [1] in deriving the richest possible
deductions from the simplest possible axioms, then the *Poco
Adagio* of this Quartet is the finest music of Brahms we have
yet studied. Run through it, and admire the ever-new light
he throws on that simple but deeply expressive cello refrain of
Figure 13, b. In the passage quoted it dominates the whole
progression, carrying us down, through the whole of page 23
of the score, from E to D, then on page 24 from D to C, and,
with briefest reference to B, back to the return of the main
theme: a whole drama motivated by one thought. In the
tragically intense theme for piano at the bottom of page 25,
on the other hand, its rôle becomes subordinate, but no less
indispensable. Put into the strings, it clinches the cadence of
each phrase, and by its powerful current carries us on into the
next; its quicker recurrence in the climax on page 26 fairly
takes our breath away. And then in the coda it once more

---

[1] Compare Bertrand Russell's essay, "The Study of Mathematics," and the
present writer's "Music and Mathematics," the latter in the volume *Music as a
Humanity*.

returns to the foreground, but now in chastened mood and with a touching tenderness of expression. All through the last page it seems bathed in that clarified shadowless light that so often makes recollection almost more vivid than experience itself; we seem to be tasting the very kernel of our feeling, hav-

Figure 14.

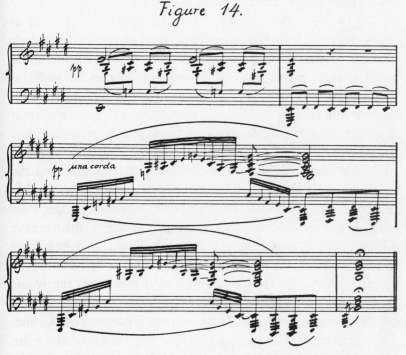

ing left its husk behind; and as the violin trills on the high E the harmony loses its restlessness as a pendulum its oscillations, and comes to rest on the central E in final equilibrium, while the piano gives a last souvenir of the smeared arpeggios. The most beautiful touch of all is reserved to the very end, the last half of the next to the last measure, where the figure reverses its direction and is inflected below the E instead of above it. (Figure 14). How beautiful is this sombre drooping from the key-note! And how immeasurably more effective, heard thus but once, than if its virtue were diluted by repetition! Only the greatest minds have this supreme artistic self-denial —to say once, and be silent.

Similarly in the first movement, despite the richness of its materials, the warmth of its instrumental coloring, despite even its towering climaxes, what proves in the long run most moving is its ineffable simplicities. There is first of all the simplicity (which the unobservant might mistake for bareness) of its principal theme, Figure 13, c. Simple as it seems, there is not a feature of it that is not capable of pregnant development, and that is not destined to grow into new meanings. The contrast of the A in the second with the A sharp in the fourth measure, already noted, opens the way during page 4 for a fine climax. The charm of the "empty accent" in the first triplet affords the cello a pleasant contrast with the more sturdy rhythm of the second theme given to the piano at the bottom of page 5, and provides in the course of it some amusing by-play for all the strings. As for the most meaningful feature of all, the contrast between three notes to the beat and two (underlined, it will be noticed, by making the three staccato and the two legato) the essence of it is of course emotional, the contrast between the energy of the triplets and the tenderer feeling of the duplets. And this contrast, amplified, provides the greater part of the development, the whole scheme of which is to begin quietly with the duplets at the bottom of page 10, and by gradually admitting the triplets, letting them loose and giving them the rein, to build up the splendid climax of the next two pages.

Yet fine as these big moments are, what we chiefly carry away is the "still small voice" of the quieter passages where we leave noise and bustle behind us and seem to penetrate to the essence of the matter. This essence is the first theme; and nothing proves better the perfection of form of the movement than the fact that its three most memorable moments are all concerned with this theme, and all concerned with it in a

mood too serene to admit much volume of sound. The first is the opening, where the theme that is to dominate the whole is stated as directly as the text of a sermon or the proposition in a mathematical problem. The second is the deliciously quiet, unpretentious return of the theme, in its original form, on the piano, in neutral sonority, at the beginning of the recapitulation (page 14), where it contrasts so happily with the turmoil just heard in the development.

The third, and the loveliest of all, as we might expect when we are dealing with Brahms, is the coda. Its gist may be condensed as in Figure 15. The points to note about it are its thematic rigor, nothing being admitted that does not either appear in the opening measure of the theme, or grow immediately out of it, and its equally rigorous truth of emotion, the last drop being here wrung from the opposition of triplets and duplets which is the essence of the musical mood. It begins with an "imitation" of the piano by the strings, after one beat and a fifth lower in pitch, that no one but a genius would have thought of, but that everyone will agree to be the one supremely right thing to do at this point. It sums up the whole atmosphere of the piece as nothing else could do. After its repetition, in somewhat fuller scoring, comes the second element, in which the quieter duplets combine with the subdominant key to deepen the shadows in the string parts, the bass of the piano only reminding us of the triplets and their vanished noonday. Last of all come the duplets in dying cadence, imitated in deepest pathos from piano to viola and then to violin and cello. With one of those elongations of rhythm so skilfully wrought by Brahms that we hardly notice them consciously, only feeling their emotional appropriateness, the last few eighth-notes stretch out into halves; and the tonic cadence, long delayed as if in languor, finally falls. . . . Then, suddenly, two beats of *forte* triplets, recalling the vigor of the theme in its prime—and the poem is complete.

CHAPTER V

THE PIANO QUINTET IN F MINOR, OPUS 34

THE great Quintet was one of the slowest of all Brahms's works to win recognition; undoubtedly it is one of the hardest of them all to understand. Its epic breadth of conception is made even more difficult to follow, especially in the first movement, by the same youthful prolixity we find in the two quartets. The scherzo, immensely effective in its rhythmic momentum, is built from three separate and distinct themes, all of which we have to remember, and to correlate in our minds, in order to grasp its evolution. The finale, with its mystical and impassioned introduction, its varied themes, each evolving within itself, and the dizzying coda in which they are combined, truly symphonic in proportions as in texture, makes severe demands on our concentrative powers. The only simple movement is the beautiful *Andante*.

Nor are we listeners the only ones to whom the Quintet presents difficulties. The composer himself had even more than his usual trouble in getting it into final and satisfactory shape. He wrote it first, in the early sixties, before going to Vienna to live, as a string quintet with two cellos. This form failing to give him the almost orchestral sonorities the musical ideas require, he turned it into the Sonata for Two Pianos that still exists as Opus 34b. When Clara Schumann insisted, however, that it imperatively demanded string tone, he set to work again to produce the version we know, in which the rhythmic incisiveness of the piano is happily combined with the singing powers of the bowed instruments.

a. Allegro, non troppo.
Violin (with Cello and Piano)   Figure. 16.

b. (All four strings)
Piano

c. Bridge

d. II.

e. III.

Although the first impression of the opening *Allegro* is of an almost baffling richness, there is fortunately no doubt about who is the hero of the drama. The main theme is as firmly held as in the A major Quartet, both in its tentative presentation in medium sonority (Figure 16, a) and in its rugged *fortissimo* form (16, b) where the full strings carry it forward, buoyed up and hurled onward by the surging waves of the piano figure underneath. But when the pensive Brahmsian bridge theme comes (16, c), beautiful as it is in itself, and ingeniously as it is prepared by the preceding cadence, it is not easy for us to keep it in its proper subordinate place, especially as its sustained, singing melody is apt at first hearing to sound more important than the almost choppy second theme (16, d). And when, having succeeded in assimilating this, we arrive at the conclusion theme (16, e) we find not one but a whole panoply of new rhythms to catch.

The development and the recapitulation continue this impression of complexity; it is only in the masterly coda that the main theme assumes the complete dominance it deserves; yet none the less, we are here far from the effects of fragmentary miscellaneity that sometimes troubled us in the quartets. The most massive changes of rhythm are now manipulated with such art-concealing art as to steal upon us almost imperceptibly, carrying us safe through the strongest contrasts. An object lesson in this new flexibility is the end of the exposition, at page 10 of the score. There we may marvel how the motive of three descending notes, in a jerky rhythm, which appeared almost casually in the conclusion theme (16, e) is first turned into even eighth-notes, repeated in Brahms's favorite manner so as to cross the bar-lines and momentarily obscure the meter, and then broadened into the group of three quarter-notes (with an "empty first beat") that end the exposition in a vein of high seriousness. One and the same motive is here pressed by the skilful composer into three very different expressive functions, and becomes in turn coy and whimsical, excitedly forward-pressing, and nobly reposeful.

The same flexibility of treatment is seen in the "preparations"; nearly every important new theme is unobtrusively but effectively prepared, usually in the cadence of the one preceding. Of all these preparations not only the most elaborate, as is fitting, but the most beautiful, is that for the

Figure 17.

recapitulation, part of which is shown in Figure 17, a. Under light chords in the ethereal higher register of the piano, syncopated in quarter-notes so as to hover tentatively over the melody and yet mark its meter unmistakably, first the second violin and viola, and then the cello, suggest in softest tones the original theme. The accompanying chords veer uncertainly between F major and F minor; and the supreme subtlety is reached when the cello reflects this uncertainty, as it were, in the theme itself, taking first A natural and then A flat as if hesitating which to choose, as if "thinking aloud" of the relative merits of both. Such recreating of the very substance of a theme is the rarest thing in music, given to only the most thoughtful composers to achieve.

Just before the coda, on page 23 of the score, we reach again the noble motive of three quarter-notes after an "empty first." This time, instead of cadencing, it is so dovetailed between piano and strings as to generate a new climax, and then to fade gradually away to the softest *pianissimo*. The first violin then begins a final series of quiet imitations, by the strings, of the main motive of the movements, now in major, over a pedal point on F in the piano. When the cello, *pianissimo*, takes up the theme in solemnly augmented rhythm (Figure 17, b), under ethereal high harmonies in the other strings, it comes as if inevitably to the same hesitation between A natural and A flat that is made memorable before, placed now even more poignantly on its singing A-string. And then, resuming the seriousness of the lowest string, it plays still further with its meditation on the theme, varying the variation we have already heard in Figure 17, a. And we feel once more the indescribable charm of this musical day-dreaming that is allowed such incomparable freedom and breadth in the music of Brahms.

After the profundities of the first movement, the lyric *Andante*, as essentially simple as a Schubert song, comes as a relief. Its swaying melody (Figure 18) in *"gemüthlich"* thirds and sixths, hesitates frequently between major and minor with a pensiveness that recalls Schubert, while the accompaniment, in which the strings reinforce the palpitating figure of the pianist's left hand, has all the delicious rhythmic subtlety of another of Brahms's favorites—Johann Strauss. The music flows quietly on in a divine leisure, like some meadow brook,

Figure 18.

now forgetting its current in eddies and pools, now passing more strongly into a cadence;—at the end broadening into the coda as into a tranquil basin of brown pebbles and golden sands. Worthy of detailed study is the elaborate and dramatically impressive preparation, following the middle section of the movement, by which, from Tempo 1 on page 31 for more than a page, the opening theme is at first dimly suggested and then at last allowed to reënter in all its quiet beauty. Observe any audience during this return, and realize how ecstatic, when the composer thoroughly shares it with the listeners, musical happiness can be!

The immense rhythmic verve of the scherzo, its relentless insistence, from the light, deliberately paced cello *pizzicati* of the opening measures to the quick-fire hammer-stroke sixteenth-notes of all the strings at the end, on the duple meter which is here used for the first time in the chamber music scherzos, may well induce us to reconsider our conclusion, apropos of the Intermezzo of the G minor Quartet, that Brahms, in contrast with Tschaikowsky, is never merely primitive. The energy of this unflagging *"One,* two, *One,* two," kept up for ten pages, or, if we include the only slightly less vigorous scoring of the trio, for twenty-three, is surely nothing less than savage. Yet merely primitive it is not; even when, as in its last pages, it is hammering pitilessly on our ears and nerves, it never fails to fascinate our minds also; and indeed the essential marvel of it is that it achieves inexhaustible variety of detail without sacrificing basic unity.

Both the unity and the variety are here so subtle that it is worth while to define them rather carefully. As we have seen in dealing with the G minor Quartet, unity in a movement of this type usually depends largely on some persistent figure in one or more parts, forming a sort of measuring rod against which rhythmic vagaries can be told off by the listening ear. In the present scherzo, the changes from 2–4 to 6–8 time and back seem, at least to the eye, to contradict this principle, but in reality they do not. They are more apparent to the eye than to the ear, which from the opening cello *pizzicato* to the machine-gun fusillade at the end gets a steady impression of two-beat measures, the beats containing sometimes three notes, sometimes four, and, in the countersubject of the little fugato, a highly piquant two. Even in the trio, the pace is only slightly relaxed, made a little more gracious, a little less insistent.

Hence, in the whole movement, a truly overwhelming uniformity of pulse.

But against this uniform metrical background, what a wealth of contrasting rhythmic silhouettes is projected! What an immeasurable distance has the composer now travelled from the early Trio with its monotonous thetic rhythms and its insecure meter! Here again the eye is a misleading guide, and causes to look alike rhythms that to the ear sound quite different. The four themes of the movement—three for the scherzo proper, and one for the trio—shown in Figure 19, are all notated in measures containing only two beats, though they are conceived in four-beat groups. The result is that the contrast between heavy and light measures is not shown the eye, however unmistakably it is perceived by the ear. Hence themes c and d, for instance, look far more alike than they sound: to reproduce to the eye the differences the ear feels we must either write them in 12–8 (and theme b in 4–4) or give distinguishing marks to the heavy (H) and the light (L) measures. If we do this we shall feel clearly the fascinating rhythmic contrasts that differentiate all four themes.

Theme a, the main theme of the scherzo, in accordance with its energetic, downright character, is strongly thetic—*i.e.*, its phrases start with accented notes—or rather, to be quite accurate, "more royalist than the king," it is more than thetic through its anticipatory syncopations. Thus its character is solid, almost heavy.

Theme b, on the other hand, suitably to its coy, half-whimsical character, begins its phrases with "empty first beats" (for each G, in each heavy measure, belongs with what precedes, not with what follows). The humor, not to say mischief, of this lightly-rhythmed theme opposes itself to the stolidity of the first as feminine tact and subtlety often oppose themselves to the automatism of masculine instinct.

Theme c, again, is vigorous—and with an even more forthright vigor than a's—with its solid steps, a note to each

Figure 19.

beat, and the triplet anacruses with which it hurls itself upon each crucial tone.

And now admire the subtlety of the contrast between c and d. They *look* much alike; they even *are* alike in their anacrustic triplets—an effective element of unification. But while c owes to its constant anacrustic hurling of itself forward much of its insatiable vigor, the opening phrase of the trio theme begins with an "empty first," and ends with a feminine cadence—in other words, is as leisurely and good-humored as the other is strenuous. With such delightful subtleties of rhythmic expression can a master star the moments even of a scherzo which seems at first merely headlong in its momentum.

In the finale the process of radically transforming a theme that we admired in the first movement is carried even further, and made more systematic, as in some uncanny Jekyll-and-Hyde experiment. What makes it here even more striking in its results is that the main theme, to which it is applied, is not in itself highly significant, is indeed almost commonplace, so that all its final significance seems to be due to the transforming power of the composer's imagination. We all remember the common round melody "Frère Jacques, Frère Jacques, Dormez-vous? Dormez-vous?", etc. Transpose it into minor, and you have the essential progressions, up from *do* through *mi* to *sol*, of Brahms's theme (Figure 20, a). This is given out *piano* by the violoncello at the beginning of the movement, accompanied by light sixteenth-notes on the piano, and presently repeated by the piano, with the sixteenth-notes in the strings. It is followed by a more sustained second theme (score, top of page 55) and by a concluding passage in strongly syncopated triplets (page 57).

So far all is in the usual finale formula. But now, before the first repetition of the main theme itself, comes its first *alter ego*, in the dominant key of C minor, and so concentrated upon its *staccato* eighth-notes as to possess a wholly new and highly piquant flavor (Figure 20, b). After this the movement again pursues its normal course of development and

repetition until it reaches the same point in the recapitulation
at which the exposition yielded this strange variant. And here
there is another variant, even stranger, and even more haunting

in its mystery and melancholy (Figure 20, c). We recognize
the same progression, to *mi*, and then to *sol*; but the atmosphere
of trivial prosaic daylight of the original theme is here replaced

by a solemn twilight and semi-darkness. The fourth and last transformation of the theme appears in the remote key of C sharp minor and with an odd rhythmic change to 6–8 time, with breathless "empty firsts," and starts off the coda on its headlong course. (Its opening measures are shown at Figure 20, d.) With its reappearance, *fortissimo*, in the home key of F minor, and in all five instruments, at page 68 of the score, the final sprint is well commenced; and from there to the end climax follows climax, on the second theme and on combinations of it with this final and most highly energized avatar of the first.

Thus all in all the Quintet is one of those crucial works we find in the careers of the greatest composers, in which old tendencies are carried to their highest point, and new ones are initiated. In its massive sonorities, its heaven-storming energy of passion and thought, it belongs with the piano quartets, and reaches the limit they suggest. It is probably the most symphonic of all Brahms's chamber music works. Yet at the same time his thought is becoming stricter and more inwardly creative; and these deeper insights suggest the possibility of a quieter and profounder style. It was in this new direction that, as a matter of fact, he next turned.

CHAPTER VI

THE SEXTET IN G MAJOR, OPUS 36

THE G major Sextet marks so strong a reaction from the style of the works immediately preceding it, especially the two quartets and quintet with piano, as to suggest a new departure, the opening up of a new vein. Brahms is here only making systematic, however, and carrying to their highest power, certain methods clearly if tentatively broached in those very works. In contrast with them, the Sextet is not only lighter and more transparent in texture; it is also far less complex, not to say lavish, in material, substituting for their sometimes confusing variety a strict, an almost severe simplicity. It is as if the abounding energy that in them was dissipated in youthful high spirits and a questing curiosity, here begins to concentrate itself into the quieter but profounder feeling of middle age; the thoughts, instead of developing by extension, now rather deepen in intensity; the music no longer foams and breaks itself up in rushing torrents; it lies quiet like a transparent mountain lake.

If we wished to account for this change in more technical terms we might attribute it primarily to the intensive study of counterpoint that Brahms had been making, partly in friendly rivalry with Joachim, partly in obedience to a profound instinct for the needs of his own genius. For counterpoint, far from being the dry and dreary study that early associations with scholastic fugues sometimes mislead us into supposing it, is in reality the most intimate and creative of all the elements of musical thought. Counterpoint might be defined as the analysis and synthesis of melodies in their mutual relationships; and since music owes to the struggles and agreements of melodies its profoundest emotional appeal (immeasurably deeper, for instance, than the appeal of harmonic or instrumental coloring), the most exciting thing in music is precisely counterpoint. The steady deepening of Brahms's expression during these years of his passionate devotion to contrapuntal study in thus the proof that his instinct was sound, and that this study was opening to him deeper and deeper doors into his own nature. In the breaking up and the recombination through counterpoint of the actual molecules of music his creative imagination is most masterfully at work. The stronger it becomes the deeper it penetrates, and the more rigorously it confines itself to one or to a few thoughts, brushing aside all else as irrelevant. In the Sextet this rigor of imagination, in earlier works operative only at supreme moments, becomes as it were normal and habitual.

Thus the whole of the first movement is evolved out of the first four notes played by the first violin, an unforgettably poetic and suggestive motive of two rising fifths superposed (see Figure 21), with such a closeness of logic that the other themes are remembered only as momentary contrasts, and the impression we carry away, instead of being of a Gothic richness, is positively Greek in its austere and noble beauty. Bare, almost poverty-stricken as this opening may at first seem (especially if we read it in the score instead of hearing it) there is not a note in it that is not skillfully planned to build up the impression of unique beauty, of indescribable individuality, that finally comes to invest it. The slow trill of the viola, for instance, which permeates in one shape or another most of the movement, is like the rustle of leaves in the forest, of waves in the ocean, in its inanimate gentleness, its friendly monotony.

The main theme itself, with its two fifths, one in the clear and sunny key of G major, the second veiled or clouded in the relative darkness of E flat, strikes at once the contrast of the cheerful and the pensive which motivates the whole movement. As it continues, the pensive droop of the second phrase, still in E flat,

Figure 21.

leads charmingly into the renewed good cheer of the gay little rising phrases touching G and high A. The last four measures, a little codetta, complete the melody with falling fourths and fifths, answering the rising fifths of the opening. Notable is the persistence of the viola figure throughout; even when, in the eleventh measure, the harmony changes to dominant, the viola, with the uncompliance of a hypnotic subject or of one

walking in his sleep, maintains its stubborn G–F sharp. . . .
By all these means, Brahms builds up an atmosphere of remote
and quiet beauty, as of a glade in some grey forest.

And if this atmosphere haunts the movement, that is because
Brahms in the fulness of his counterpoint-awakened imagination, sees so deeply into this theme that he need resort, save
casually, to no other. Wonderful is the development section,
with its *tour de force* of contrapuntal skill by which instrument
after instrument is made to bring the motive, sometimes as at
first, sometimes inverted with its fifths moving downward.
Wonderful are such sudden contrasts of color—sudden yet so
logical as to seem inevitable,—as that which plunges the theme,
on page 12 of the score, from the clearness of D major into a
dim ripple of C sharp minor. Wonderful, in the coda, is the
simple substitution of D sharp for the similar sounding E flat
in the motive, by which its whole course and harmony are
changed, as the legendary pebble on the Rocky Mountains
makes one stream flow east and another west. But more wonderful than any or all of these details is the plastic power by
which the composer generates them all from a single idea, thus
endowing the whole movement with unity and a noble simplicity.

The most extraordinary feature of the scherzo, which continues the experiment in duple metres begun in the Quintet,
is the uncanny mastery of counterpoint it displays—the ability
to take a few scraps, like those odd bits of cotton or silk or
velvet out of which our grandmothers used to concoct "crazy
quilts", and make of them a scherzo and trio, in the traditional
form, in which you can detect nowhere a patch, and hardly a
seam. The best way to appreciate the degree of this skill for
oneself is to take the miniature score, number the measures,
and examine from one to the next how the motives are dovetailed in. Thus the scherzo proper consists of three Parts: the

Statement of themes, beginning in G minor, cadencing in the dominant, D minor, on page 29; the "Contrast", beginning at the "second ending" on the same page, and running to the fifth measure on page 31; and the Return, beginning there and closing on page 33 before the entrance of the Trio, *Presto giocoso*. So far, so good; the marvel begins when we note how Brahms derives all the material to realize this design from two brief motives, by means of such traditional contrapuntal devices as "augmentation", "diminution", "inversion", "shifted rhythm", and the like,—and all so easily and naturally that we might enjoy it without knowing how it was done, unless we thought it worth while to find out. That it is worth while, the following tabular view and brief comments may perhaps show.

Statement. Theme I (Figure 22, a), in G minor. Note that in rhythm it is "thetic" (beginning on the accented beat), but by means of rhetorical accents it agreeably complicates the rhythm, emphasizing the up-beats.

Measures 11–12. Theme II (Figure 22, e) is already "prepared" by the violins, though it does not enter for a few bars yet.

Measure 17. Theme II in full, in D minor. At its conclusion it is imitated by the cello, while the first violin and viola play an *inversion* of Theme I, in shifted rhythm. (Figure 22, b).

Measure 25. That Themes I and II have been planned from the first to go together we here see (Theme I is inverted: Figure 22, c).

The first page or so of the contrast is made from the little figure of two notes generated from the cadence at bar 31. Note that rhythmically this has an "empty first beat". The result is that the whole of this page contrasts delightfully with the thetic rhythms of both the themes.

At measure 51 the opening measures of the two themes are combined in a new figure, elaborately imitated.

Measure 58. A fascinating "preparation" for the return of Theme I, in clear and high major sonorities.

Measure 62. The cadence measures of I provide the viola

Figure 22.

with a little motive that carries over by delightfully unconventional modulation to

Return. Page 31 (measure 70). This time things are so altered that both themes come in the tonic, and there is a coda made on a *diminution* (Figure 22, d) of Theme I.

The trio, *Presto giocoso*, we need not analyze in quite so much detail. Note however that the loud and almost bumptious form of peasant dance (Figure 22, f) is set off against a soft and as it were timid form of the same melody (Figure 22, g) made simply by *diminishing* it from four measures to two; and that its contrast, at the middle of page 34, is *inverted* at the middle of 35. Our interest in all these details is of course not for themselves, which would be pedantic, but rather in order

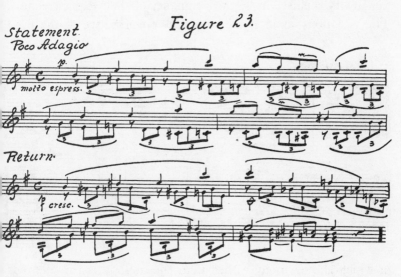

Figure 23.

to see with what supreme artistic economy Brahms can now build up a complex, various, and delightfully spontaneous piece.

It is in the variations of the *Poco Adagio*, however, that these polyphonic methods attain their greatest reach, and give to the music a spirituality, a contemplative depth, which we shall find elsewhere only in the later quartets of Beethoven. This set of variations is not only an extraordinary technical feat for a composer in his early thirties; in the spirit that lies behind the notes it shows a mature serenity that makes it one of the greatest movements anywhere in Brahms. The theme itself, in simple ternary form of Statement, Contrast, Return, is strikingly original in harmonic treatment, and of a lovely touching

plaintiveness of feeling. Here are its Statement and Return
(Figure 23). The subtlety of the chromatic inflections is
equalled, it will be noticed, by the boldness of the confrontation of E minor and D minor in the Statement, and of the use
of F major, and even minor, in the Return; and these temerities justify themselves by the poignancy of their expressiveness.
The variations, as in Beethoven's later works, are of the kind

Figure 24.

in which the harmony rather than the melody is the element
retained. In the ecstatically beautiful *Adagio* which closes the
movement, the time values are doubled in such a way that each
harmony is given new weight, without the sense of the original
movement being compromised; the chords seem to reveal
the quintessence of their meaning, as in the E major section
of the *Adagio* of Beethoven, opus 127.

In Figure 24 is transcribed the Return in the second variation, a characteristic Brahmsian scheme of antiphony between
the upper instruments and the second cello. Here a still
deeper meaning is squeezed from the modulation into F minor,
and there is an accent of earnest and nobly-enduring stoicism
to find the like of which we must turn to the setting of "Herz-
lich thut mich verlangen," No. 9 of the very last work, the

posthumously published *Choral-Vorspiele*. Thus Brahms anticipates for a moment in early manhood the full, sweet tenderness of ripest years.

The finale is a delightfully exuberant *Poco Allegro* on a broad melody in G major, which serves to end the sextet in heartiest good cheer.

II

YOUNG MANHOOD

FACSIMILE OF FIRST PAGE OF THE C MINOR STRING QUARTET

(Courtesy of the *Gesellschaft der Musikfreunde*, Vienna.)

The only actual change to be observed is the substitution of E flat, in the sixth measure of the violoncello part, for a C first written; and this was probably only a slip of the pen, as the line of the cello part was obviously planned at the start to go down through E flat to C. The chief interest of this autograph, aside from one of sentiment, is its revelation of the speed with which Brahms wrote, and of his habit of grouping a number of details into a single act. The time signature 3–2, for example, made in the violin part with two strokes of the pen, requires in the other parts, as he gets "warmed up," only a single one each. The way of making the last half-note on the first line of the viola part (*Bratsche*) is characteristic. He does not lift the pen between the two strokes needed for the two sides of the note. Consequently it crosses its own line, and only at a little distance, in its total effect, looks like a half-note. This labor-saving swiftness may be constantly observed in Brahms's manuscripts.

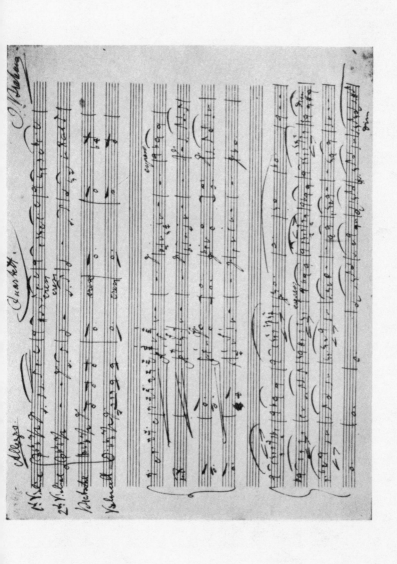

CHAPTER VII

THE CELLO SONATA IN E MINOR, OPUS 38

THE E minor Cello Sonata is the first of the seven sonatas for piano with solo instruments (two with cello, three with violin, two with clarinet) that Brahms considered worthy of preservation. In the tenth volume of the edition of his Complete Works issued by the *Gesellschaft der Musikfreunde* in Vienna there is also a scherzo for piano and violin, part of a sonata written in collaboration for Joachim in 1853 by Schumann, Brahms, and Dietrich. It is in his youthful style and was only published posthumously, in 1906, by the *Deutsche Brahms-gesellschaft*. Thus the Cello Sonata, which appeared as early as 1866, with a dedication to Joseph Gänsbacher, professor of Singing at the Vienna *Akademie*, is Brahms's earliest published essay in the solution of the special problems involved in writing for two instruments.

We need look no further than the first theme of the first movement to realize that a sound instinct led him to adopt melodic imitation between the two instruments, based often on the double counterpoint in which he had attained such skill, as the norm of an appropriate style: the piano imitates the cello theme at the twenty-first measure, while the cello continues with a bass melody written in flowing double counterpoint. In the immediate continuation the give-and-take between the two instruments turns into a quick dialogue, not to say exchange of repartee; and all through the bridge over to the second theme there is plenty of imitation. In the second theme itself the imitation becomes even more headlong, taking place "across the meter", in the peculiar Brahmsian hobbling rhythm, as may be shown in short-hand reduction of its opening bars thus:

Figure 25.

What is more, with the rhythmic freedom he has now attained Brahms is able, when the same imitations recur in softer mood and mysterious low register between the two hands of the piano, to introduce in their course (see Figure 26) unexpected pauses that indescribably deepen their emotional appeal. All this is highly effective. The eloquent lower register of the cello is tellingly used, the burden of the melody running largely there rather than in the higher voices entrusted to the less

singing piano tone. Even the piano, for that matter, is made
to put its best foot forward in those lovely fresh major
harmonies of the conclusion theme; and its anacrustic use of
the two-note motive is subtly opposed to the cello's dreamful

Figure 26.

harping on the thetic version of the same falling interval of
a fifth. This passage is especially lovely when it recurs in E
major, in extended form and with rich modulations, at the
close of the movement.

Yet the piano and the violoncello are not, after all, truly

well-balanced running mates; the cello, despite the nobility of its singing voice, is even less capable of holding its own with the piano in *fortes* and *fortissimos* than the violin; and beautiful as are its basses in this sonata, Brahms puts it at an unnecessary disadvantage by keeping it in its lower register almost continually. When we reflect how seldom even the piano quartets and quintet, where there are three or four bowed instruments to hold up their end, are played as true ensemble works, how painfully usual it is to treat them as piano virtuoso pieces with string backgrounds, we tremble for the delicate tissue of this duet. Nine out of ten pianists, as we all know to our sorrow, are egotistical or insensitive enough to turn the most hopeful chamber music democracies into tyrant-ridden dictatorships. And the modern grand piano, as a mechanism, is so many times too powerful for its more sensitive companions, that even the few pianists with enough sense of balance, ability to hear themselves as others hear them, and preference of art to virtuosity, to gear their instruments down as they need, find that to do so takes the rarest native intelligence and trained skill. So that one would wish that composers, especially those who understand these problems of balance as subtly as Brahms, would never put temptation in their way, but would always write piano parts that not only can be played right, but cannot be played wrong.

When, consequently, in the fugal finale of this sonata, we find Brahms adopting a highly contrapuntal style, in which all voices are significant and must often therefore be equal, and demanding of the cello (still written rather low) that it hold its own with its more percussive and athletic brother, now unleashed to all the enthusiasms of a contrapuntal game of tag, we scent trouble ahead. The kernel of a fugue, especially of a triple fugue like this, or a quadruple one like that in the finale of Mozart's Jupiter Symphony, is usually to be found about two thirds or three quarters of the way through. In this case it comes thirty-nine bars before the *Piu Presto*, at the return of the tonic, E minor, after the long dominant pedal-point. It consists, first, of the main theme, which we may call A, with its vigorous downward octave jump followed by scurrying triplets, played by piano, right hand; second, of a countersubject that originally appeared in the piano in the fifth measure, and that is now entrusted to the cello—a debonair, almost saucy tune that we may call B; and finally of C, a rather lumbering theme (piano, left hand) built on the Brahms "Leit-motive," and provided with plenty of trills and slurs across the beats to make it hug the ground. Now powerful as the musical thoughts and their contrapuntal combination may be here, as mere sound they leave a good deal to be desired. For when you set a single cello to competing like this with the two hands of an able-bodied pianist, giving him no handicaps, the odds are certainly on the pianist. And when in other sections your poor cellist takes either of the other two themes, he is apt to resemble, in theme C, a playful whale, and in A, with its busy triplets scuttling in the deep bass, a rather more strenuous "denizen of the deep", say a porpoise, vainly endeavoring to escape from a particularly dark and muddy aquarium. The only times he comes up to breathe are the lyrical episodes, made with extraordinary contrapuntal and rhythmic skill from the two countersubjects; here he is allowed to sustain harmonies or sing melodies, and the sound improves accordingly.

But if Brahms can be thus momentarily felicitous, not to say charming, even in the fugue, in the *Allegretto quasi Menuetto*, and especially in its trio, he shows himself a lover of delicious sounds for their own sakes, and a past master in devising them. The figuration is here in the best Schumann tradition, with its whimsical dips in the right hand against the steady support of the left. Its use of dissonant notes on the accents (neighbors instead of members of the harmonies) gives its melody the same plangency of sound and delicate urgency of movement as that of "Des Abends"; its pauses and hesitancies are as poetic as Schumann's, its rhythms even subtler than his.

Minuet and trio alike are built from a motive of the greatest charm, even as we hear it first, and constantly increasing its fascination under the tonal and especially the rhythmic development given it. It is the dominant note, E, of A minor, accompanied by its upper and then its lower neighboring note (Figure 27, a). It is plaintive; and its plaintiveness is increased by its phrasing (the upward inflection D to E slurred) and much more subtly by its rhythmic placing in a light measure, so that its entire six notes are anacrustic to the A of the cello. The important structural facts that the motive is beginning with four full beats of anacrusis, and that the first full measure is therefore not a heavy but a light, is unmistakably conveyed by the composer to the sensitive hearer by the "lie" of the chief cello melody, and by the harmonic basis, which Brahms always uses to clarify difficult or especially interesting rhythms: we cannot hear five measures without feeling that the heavy accents come on the A's of the cello. This is corroborated and intensified by the first half-note, in the tenth measure, and another one two measures further on. (Notice that Brahms is here making his cadence from the motive itself, letting it end now on the suspensive note E instead of the more assertive A, and emphasizing this E by several repetitions.) The piano, repeating what the cello has said, then brings the first Part of the minuet to an end. To usher in the second Part, the C in the motive is changed to C sharp, and all the harmonies are inflected accordingly (Figure 27, b). This second half is longer, and even introduces a new motive in C minor; but what above all makes it memorable is the fascinating extension by which Brahms so alters its lingering descents to the A that in the last one the

Figure 27.

* *Heavy measure.*

piano presents the motive, for the first time, on a *heavy* measure! The charm of this change, so simple yet so far-reaching, could never be described. It must be felt, and felt many times, until it sinks into our hearts (Figure 27, c).

Certainly one of the secrets of the charm is the gradualness, and yet the logical inevitability, with which the progressive changes steal over the central motive; and this charm continues to increase all through the trio. Why, for instance, we ask ourselves, does the pensiveness, which is only coy in the minuet, become almost pathetic in the opening of the trio shown at Figure 28, a? Were we dealing with a less imaginative composer we might exhaust the reasons by remarking the Schumannesque figuration, as we have already done, the sensuous beauty given by the dissonances, the freely flowing movement of the melody, perhaps adding a word on the brighter color of F sharp minor after A minor. With Brahms all these attractions are present, but they are all superficial compared to the deep beauty of the continuous flowering of the musical thought. Thus at the beginning of the trio, having already accented the lower neighboring note in his motive by placing it, at the end of the minuet, on a heavy measure, Brahms begins to dwell on it. He abbreviates the motive to four notes, of which this neighbor is the next to the last. He raises it to a *chromatic* instead of a diatonic neighbor (B sharp instead of plain B) thereby greatly increasing its sensitiveness. He sounds the little sighing four-note figure three times, with pauses that allow it to sink into our minds. This three-fold repetition is truly the most poignant addition of all, for it means that we have here, and twice more when it recurs, the only three-measure phrases among all the two-measure phrases of this entire piece.

When he comes to the end of the first Part in his trio, he does not cadence positively, but oscillates once more, as if uncertain, on another three-measure group of motives. Then, applying the principle of modified repetition in a manner as delightful as it is unexpected, he sails off on the same melody as before, harmonized now in A major instead of in F sharp minor (the opening only of this second Part is shown in Figure

8, b). Finally, when he comes to the end of this second half, he sounds the sighing figures in their three-measure phrase once more (the first three measures of Figure 28, c) and then,

Figure 28

in the only moment where the pathos takes on a touch of passion, lets the cello sing an eloquent cadence, ending strongly in F sharp minor. *Here for the first time the four-note motive becomes thetic rather than anacrustic;* and it is the synchronizing of its opening note with the measure accent that gives it here such a novel force.

Let the student now look back over the main adventures of this four-note motive as summarized in our figures. Let him even refresh his memory by a short-hand notation something like this:

Figure 27, a. Motive in A minor, anacrustic, on a light measure, with diatonic lower neighboring note.

Figure 27, b. Motive in A *major*.

Figure 27, c. Transferred, in the third measure from the end, to a *heavy* measure.

Figure 28, a. With a chromatic neighboring note, heard three times, with pauses, in a three-measure phrase. Then starting a melody on fifth step of F sharp minor.

Figure 28, b. Starting a melody as third step in A major.

Figure 28, c. Becoming thetic, and its two beats repeated three times in two measures of three beats each.

Then let him forget all this analyzing, listen once more to the whole piece, and rejoice in the inexhaustible resources of the musical imagination, and the endless beauties it reveals.

CHAPTER VIII

THE TRIO FOR VIOLIN, HORN, AND PIANO, OPUS 40

THERE are in the world of chamber music few more completely satisfying, more unforgettable experiences than the opening theme of Brahms's Horn Trio. For many of us the first hearing of it remains all our lives a sort of symbol of all that is most romantic in music. As those palpitating and pure tones of the horn steal upon our ears, with their poignant insistence, their plangent melancholy, it is as if we heard them through some forest glade; common surroundings fade away, and we can easily fancy ourselves with the composer on those "wooded heights among fir-trees" near Baden-Baden where, as he afterwards told a friend, this theme first came to him. Exquisite is the quietude of the first phrase (Figure 29, a), sung first by the violin, then in the full clear tones of the horn. More poignant, especially after the solemn hollow octaves of the piano circling about B flat, is its continuation in higher register. Most poignant of all is its final phrase (Figure 29, b) rising to a cry of pain and then falling slowly to silence. It is unlike any other melody in music, this crying and sighing of the horn on tones whose sadness seems to be only the greater the more it is expressed.

This melody is quintessentially horn music; it could hardly have been conceived for any other instrument; even when we play it on the piano, our mind's ear hears it sung by the horn. An instrument is like a person in its unalterable individuality.

Figure 29.

The horn is a somewhat crusty eccentric. Constitutionally incapable of the flexibility of the flute, the fluent agility of the clarinet, the versatility and universal adaptability of the violin, it yet atones for all shortcomings by its manly sturdiness, its deep and poetic heart. Treat it with tact and understanding, demand from it only what it can give, and it will reveal to you all its golden sweetness.

The fundamental mechanical limitation of the natural horn, the ancestor and character-determining progenitor of the modern valve-horn, is that its tones are formed by the lips of the player causing to vibrate in different subdivisions an air-column of fixed length, and hence are distributed rather peculiarly throughout its range. For example, the so-called "open tones", produced by differences of wind pressure alone, without "stopping" by the hand of the player, in the E flat horn used in this trio, are shown at Figure 30, a; and it will be seen at a glance that in the lower part of the range they lie rather far apart, but increasingly near together as they ascend. The player of the natural horn is thus, to quote a witty comparison of Cecil Forsyth's, like a man trying to climb a ladder of which the lower rungs are so wide apart that he can hardly reach from one to the other, while the upper ones are so close together that he can scarcely get his feet between them. It is true that even with the natural horn it was possible by means of the hand to produce certain so-called "stopped tones" which (though they were of different quality) filled up many of the gaps in the natural series, and that the valves made it possible to produce all the tones of the chromatic scale through a large part of the range; but these were, so to speak, later superficial modifications, overlying but not altering the fundamental character of the instrument.

Now it will not surprise us to find Brahms, whom we have already seen to have the most sensitive appreciation of the peculiar powers and limitations of the piano, treating with extraordinary sensitiveness an instrument which always occupied a peculiar place in his affections, and for which he conceived such unforgettable passages as the main themes of the Second

Symphony and the B flat Piano Concerto, and the Alpine call
in the finale of the First Symphony. And if we glance at the
opening theme of the trio once more, or at the themes of the
scherzo and of the finale shown at Figure 30, b and c, we shall
note with interest that his melodies do reflect in general the

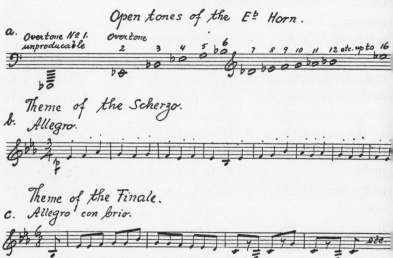

Figure 30.

Open tones of the E♭ Horn.

Theme of the Scherzo.

Theme of the Finale.

odd distribution of tones in the natural series: above the E flat
on the first line of the staff they move mostly step-wise; below
it they contain wider jumps. And furthermore it is unmistakable that this peculiar disposition and movement gives them
much of their specific "horn-call" quality.

Again, the simple technical fact that in the horn increasing
tension of the player's lips produces, by increasing subdivision
of the vibrating air-column, higher and higher tones, gives
to mere rise in pitch an emotional intensity it can never have
in instruments which like the piano produce different pitches
by means of different strings. Where pitch rises through the

continually increasing tension of a single string, as in the violin or the voice, or of a single air-column, as in the horn, we feel by sympathy a unique emotional intensification. Of this Brahms fully avails himself in his main theme. Our own throats tighten when in its second half the melody raises its starting-point from F to A flat; and when at its climax it rises to the B flat, and even to the C (rendered more poignant too as that is by the dissonance in the harmony), the tension becomes almost painful. Throughout the trio Brahms uses masterly art and self-control in this adjustment of tension. Only twice in the whole work does he touch the highest note, E flat; once at the most passionate moment of the dramatic *Adagio*, and once again on the last page but one, in the coda of the finale. The low, relaxed tones are used with similar economy.

Equally striking is the nicety of his adjustment between the open and the closed tones, especially in the pivoting of the melodies on certain central or controlling ones, illustrated again in the main theme. The horn player, it must be remembered, does not simply strike, as the pianist does, a tone ready-made for him: he has to prepare his tone before he sounds it, and this not only with his lips and hands but with his mind: he has in fact to "think" it. Hence the melodies he finds most natural and easy are those with a sort of armature of recurring tones, mostly open, about which the less important ones, many of them "closed", cling as flesh to bones, or as ivy to a tree. It is amusing to note how closely Brahms's tunes follow this pattern. The very first measure of the first theme illustrates the point clearly, if on a small scale. The fact that the E natural, the neighboring note used as subsidiary to the F, is a closed tone, while the F itself is open, subordinates it in just the right way, puts it in the background physically as well as mentally, and so gives the melody a natural shapeliness and expressiveness. Brahms himself recognized to the full the importance of the natural chiaroscuro of open and closed tones. "If the player were not compelled to blend his open notes with his closed ones," he once said, "he would never learn to blend his tone in chamber music at all."

Finally, the same sympathy with the instrument is conspicuously shown in the shaping of the rhythms. There is about the tone of the horn a natural weightiness which fits it especially for accentuation, for the marking of the salient moments of the rhythms, especially when it dominates, as it does here, instruments of less richly nourished tone like the piano and even the violin. See how shrewdly these qualities are turned to use in the opening melody. The open F's, and later the open C's, sturdy quarter-notes, are not only relieved against less prominent notes, lightened by eighth-note movement, but are planted firmly on the heavy beats of the measures. During these heavy beats even the bass, the most important harmonic part, is empty; it is on the light beats that the piano completes the harmonies. In the themes of the scherzo and the finale we see a gayer but equally idiomatic type of horn melody: the pivotal tones on the main accents form a very simple armature or framework; easily reached neighbors variegate the unaccented parts of the measures. The tunes are therefore easy to think, and easy to play.

It may be objected that some of these felicities, whatever their effect on the valveless horn, will be lost on the horn with valves, and therefore hardly concern the modern listener. Some critics have carried the same point to the extent of blaming Brahms for writing the horn parts in his symphonies as if for natural horns, and have called him an old fogey who could not keep up with the times. In answer it may be said that while Brahms may have been sometimes over-conservative, his method seems on the whole more fruitful than that of fanatic modernists who brush away the past as so much "old junk." The old natural horn, with its crooks to determine its general pitch, and for that matter the older hunting horn itself, without even a crook, exists within the modern valve horn, and cannot be forgotten without impoverishing our sense of that instrument, and vulgarizing our way of writing for it. While it is true, therefore, that the modern horn is so agile that it can play "almost anything," to write this almost anything for it, as if it were a flute or a clarinet, is not to enrich music but to impoverish it by the loss of one of its most individual voices. To "modernize" thus is to annul rather than to emancipate. Such a fallacy is like that of the simplified-spelling crank, who takes a word like, let us say, "almighty," full of the rich deposits of ages, and by spelling it "almity" destroys at a stroke all these enriching associations. Hearing such a word, our unconscious minds no longer savor the fact that almighty is something full of "might," that might is like "macht," power to "make," and that one almighty is one who can make all. No, all this is annihilated, and a silly empty word like "almity" alone remains. So is it with too many sentimental chromatic modern passages for horn. Why should they be written for horn at all? They forget its history, its character, its style, its very personality.

With Brahms, on the contrary, the actual molecules and atoms of the music are shaped by the instrument it is conceived for—the motives reach our ears as if from the ancient forest rather than the modern concert hall. What is more, the character of the instrument affects even the form of the richly romantic first movement. The sonata-form is not used, because its opposition and development of two equal themes would be too dramatic and too complex. A sectional plan is adopted instead, allowing the presentation three times, in varying keys and settings, of the chief theme, with alternations, for the sake of contrast, of an entirely subordinate theme of more restless character *("Poco piu animato")*. Thus the noble horn melody is given space to expand in deliberately, dominates the entire movement, and imparts to it a character singularly majestic and monumental.

One cannot help wondering whether the stately character of the horn may not also have suggested a peculiar feature of the scherzo—the passage in B major, at page 18 of the score, in which the theme is held up at every third note for a whole measure, while the piano fills out the harmony. Tovey, who tells us that Joachim took this section at exactly the tempo of all the rest, not holding it back in the way that has become traditional, states that this way of augmenting a theme was here used for the first time, although he adds that it became a characteristic of Brahms's later style. Only a special method of applying that contrapuntal analysis and synthesis of themes which we have already noted in the Quintet, it is indeed frequently used from this time on.

The *Adagio mesto* is one of the most profoundly felt and one of the most subtly composed of all the slow movements of Brahms. Its opening theme (first four measures of Figure 31), solo for piano in the sombre lower register, might in the depth of its contemplativeness be taken from one of the later intermezzi; it strikes at once the note of pondering and of pain that sounds through the whole movement. It is followed at the fifth measure, and completed, by a more impassioned melody for violin. Contrasted with both of these is a third element, a strangely mystical, inert motive in even eighth-notes, sounded *piano legato* at the nineteenth measure by horn, imitated by violin and later by piano. Utterly contrasted as this motive at first seems with the pondering passion of the main theme, it has really been conceived as a countersubject to it, and accompanies it at the recapitulation in a passage of lofty beauty.

Toward the close of the movement comes the first experiment in the chamber music towards a preparation which, over-
leaping the boundaries of a single movement, partakes of

Figure 31.

yclism—that permeation of a whole work by one theme that
makes it a true cycle. We remember what the finale theme is
to be—the gay *do, re, mi, sol,* horn call, in warmest E flat
major, shown in Figure 30, c. The slow movement has so
far, however, been veiled and muffled in its tonal atmosphere
—mostly E flat minor and G flat major. It is therefore as if
clouds and heavy mists evaporated before a late autumnal sun
when the E flat minor cadence of the violin theme suddenly
turns to major and the horn sounds quietly but in clearest
major the tones that are presently to dominate the finale.

Figure 32.

This leads to a magnificent outburst of the violin theme itself, now for the first time in major and in high register, and on that climax, and its subsidence to mystery, the movement ends.

The finale is as gay and as tireless as a little river that winds through the meadows of a gently sloping valley. It bubbles into ever-new rhythms, it foams with charming arabesques, it pounds with the reiterated notes of the horn. If it is never broken into rapids, neither does it ever lie in stagnant pools. Indeed it hardly forms a single eddy from its careless buoyant beginning to its triumphant close.

CHAPTER IX

THE QUARTET IN C MINOR, OPUS 51, NO. 1

CHRONOLOGY is not always very illuminating, especially in the case of a composer who, like Brahms, usually kept a manuscript by him several years before publishing it, and whose extraordinary artistic scrupulousness led him to finish his C minor Piano Quartet only after sixteen years, his first Symphony only after twenty-two, and to make the definitive version of his first chamber music work only a few years before his death. Nevertheless no aid, even the comparatively external one of chronology, is to be lightly disregarded in the interesting but difficult task of forming for ourselves a clear picture of so many-sided a mass of work as his chamber music in its entirety. Up to his thirtieth year (May, 1863) he was obviously either expressing his romantic exuberance or making the studies that were to take him beyond it (Opus 8 Trio, D minor Piano Concerto, Piano Quartets and Quintet, Serenades for orchestra, Opus 11 and 16, and the first Sextet). The decade of his thirties (1863–1873) is that of the young master: —Haydn Variations, second Sextet, first Cello Sonata, Horn Trio, first two String Quartets. The mature master fills the decade from forty to fifty with beauty in richest profusion: the first two symphonies and the two overtures, the third Quartet, the first Violin Sonata, the first Viola Quintet. After 1883 we have the works of ripest art but declining energy, of which in the chamber music the great representative is the Clarinet Quintet.

What all this shows unmistakably, so far as the quartets are concerned, is the caution with which he approached them, his evident sense that they constituted the most exacting of all the types of chamber music. Before he attempts their pitilessly transparent texture he gets his hand in with two piano quartets and a quintet, and on the side of pure contrapuntal writing with two sextets. He told a friend that before Opus 51 he had already composed over twenty quartets and more than a hundred songs, adding: "It is not hard to compose, but what is fabulously hard is to leave the superfluous notes under the table." Tovey suggests that he must have experienced "extraordinary difficulty in reducing his massive harmony and polyphony to the limits of four solo strings."

Internal evidence seems to bear out Tovey's interpretation of the precise nature of the difficulty, rather than the more popular but superficial one that Brahms was indifferent to sensuous beauty, or maladroit in attaining it. It is true that the musical ideas came first in his mind, their instrumental investiture second: we remember how his Piano Quintet was first conceived as a string quintet (with two cellos), and later as a sonata for two pianos; the D minor Piano Concerto also went through the Two-piano-sonata stage, after commencing life as a symphony. Whenever, on the other hand, Brahms writes for special instruments like the horn or the clarinet, he shows an exacting sense for their most delicate and individual nuances of tone and articulation. Moreover even when he is writing for the more common instruments (such for instance as the piano, the commonest of all) his feeling is most keen, as we have noticed in the G minor Quartet, for recasting his ideas in precisely the idiom congenial for each. Finally, no less experienced and sensitive a musician than Adolfo Betti, leader of the famous Flonzaley Quartet, has said that at his best Brahms's instinct for strings is well-nigh incomparable. . . . No, Tovey seems to have put his finger on the impediment Brahms encountered in approaching the quartet: it was the "massive harmony and polyphony" of his earlier musical ideas themselves—that side of his own mind which was youthful, exuberant, excessive. And the real difficulty was one of thought. It was to bring his mind into a new focus, to make effective that clear, lucid, strict side of it that was no less vital than the exuberant one; to turn away from diffuseness to concentration, from romantic miscellaneity to classic singleness of purpose; to stop piling up Gothic cathedrals like the quartets and quintet with piano, and chisel instead those Parthenons that are the quartets for strings.

Since the natural limit of the classic concentration and inner unfolding of a few ideas might seem to be cyclism, we might expect the quartets to be strongly cyclic. In art, however, it is dangerous to push logic to extremes; the instinct of the composer is wiser than the reasonings of the analyst; and while the first quartet is indeed strongly cyclic, and the third has cyclic elements, the second, though no less closely wrought than its companions, has of cyclism hardly any trace. In the C minor Quartet all the movements except the *Allegretto*, the light movement of the four, such as is always apt to be treated as an intermezzo in the serious business of a quartet, are dominated by a single idea, or rather by the opposition between two motives of contrasting expression which forms, dramatically speaking, one idea. Just as in the Jupiter Symphony and many other works of Mozart an energetic and a pathetic motive are set to struggle with each other (a plan eagerly seized upon and carried to its expressive limit by Beethoven), so in each of these three movements a rising motive suggesting indomitable will is set in opposition with a falling one of tenderest sensibility. These elements are shown in most summary possible form in Figure 33.

The melodic style is striking for its simplicity, and for its resulting universality. Not merely is it free now from any essential turns, or over-obvious cadences recalling operatic

Figure 33.

Cyclical Motives in the C minor Quartet.

The energetic (rising) motives   The pathetic (falling) motives.

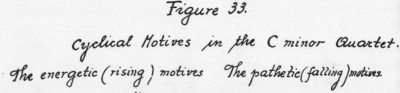

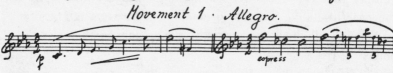

airs, or other elements alien to it, but in eliminating all such irrelevancies it has clarified itself until its texture is as straightforward, as rugged, as diatonic, as that of German folksong itself. *Do, re, mi,* in minor or major as the case may be (minor in the first and last movements, major in the *Poco Adagio*)— that is all there is to the main motive. The complementary motive begins at the other end of the scale, the upper *do,* and falls to *sol* through either *la* or *si.* Thus both motives arise out of the commonest of all chords, the tonic triad, and follow the most familiar of all paths, the diatonic scale. "It is by means of familiar words", says Joubert, "that style takes hold of the reader. . . . It is by means of these that great thoughts get currency and pass for true metal." For the rest, Brahms depends for his expressiveness, as his habit is, chiefly on rhythm. Contrast the first theme of the opening allegro with its cyclic brother of the finale, and see what amplitude and deliberation the triple measure gives it, how much more abrupt and peremptory it becomes in duple time. Feel the loving, sighing hesitancy of the sensitive motive in the *Adagio*, with all those "empty firsts" to start the beats. And note the plaintiveness the anacruses give the similar motive in the finale.

If now we open the score, we find a drama of will overpowering all the protests of the suffering soul—a struggle that recalls Schopenhauer's tragic sense of the restlessness, and at the same time the insatiability, of the will. On the very first page we have the two opposing elements unmistakably sketched in: the assertive one in the first two lines, shown in the first ten measures of Figure 34; the pleading one in the following two lines, four measures of which are shown in the figure. One notices the skill with which the original motive is not forgotten even during the contrast, but takes subordinate place in viola and second violin. At the middle of page 2 the descending motive is expanded into a true second theme. The entire movement—exposition, development, and recapitulation—is devoted to portraying the struggle of the two elements. It is the more energetic theme that triumphs, first tentatively through pages 6 and 7, and in the coda definitively. There its relentlessness is made to culminate in hammer-like blows, insistently repeated (change from three-beat to two-beat meter), until in the last dozen measures the cello carries it down to exhaustion, still essentially undefeated.

It is only in the *Poco Adagio* that this theme, by one of

Figure 34.

those magical changes of which only music is capable, takes on a new warmth, even sensitiveness, without losing its strength. (Theme I, in Figure 35.) Lovely, in its course, is the momentary change of color from richest A flat to clearest C major for two short measures (13 and 14), followed by the serious quietude of the original dominant. And how eloquent, and at the same time how nobly reticent and free from sentimentality, is its cadence, hovering on that subdominant seventh chord with fourth step raised (marked with a cross in the figure) which in places like this is so dear to Brahms as to become almost an obsession! In the breathless middle section in A flat minor (Theme II in Figure 35) with its richly sensitive harmony and its poignant rhythmic hesitations, Brahms attains an incomparable originality: who else, before or since, has been able to make music sigh as it does here? Through pages 16 and 17 this mood becomes ever more tenderly sad. Then a beautiful "preparation" of six measures, in which the

Figure 35.

pulsating rhythm is gradually dissipated, while the stronger
rhythm of the first theme slowly reasserts itself, leads into a
resumption of that theme, now in the three lower instruments,
with the first violin weaving garlands above.

But it is on the last page of the movement, bringing it to a
nobly quiet conclusion, that we find the supreme example of
the simplicity that experience has brought to the formerly
tempestuous Brahms. The middle theme was appealing enough
before; now its quintessence seems to have been distilled
into eleven haunting measures. These are followed by exactly
eleven more, devoted to the main theme. In this final embodi-
ment the completely satisfying condensation of its musical
meaning, the organ-like richness of its sound, seem almost
incredible when, after scanning it on the printed page (Coda,
in Figure 35), we hear it actually sung by the strings. For
the paradox of string quartet texture is that while the more
complex the writing the more poverty-stricken it usually sounds,
a few triads, artfully placed, produce an overpowering effect.
Such is the case here; and no one who has heard those sinuous
lines of the violins, supported by the sombre viola and given
rhythmic life by the plucked cello chords, is likely ever to
forget it.

The *Allegretto molto moderato* is one of those movements,
like the intermezzi of the G minor Piano Quartet and of the
great Quintet, where the composer momentarily relaxes tension
by playing with a hypnotically insistent meter against which
rhythmic figures flit with the irresponsibility of dreams. In
the *"lusingando"* passage the triplets introduce a pleasant
feeling of leisure. On the return of the theme they are blended
with it in a thoroughly Brahmsian manner, and the viola seems
for the first time frankly to take the lead it has been coquetting
with from the beginning.

The trio exploits an amusing special effect in the second

violin. If you play alternate A's on the open string (indicated in the score by a small circle) and the D string stopped with the finger, you get an effect not unlike that of the "warwhoop" children delight in when they sing "Ah" and slap their mouths with the palms of their hands: "Ah-oo, Ah-oo, Ah-oo", etc.

Figure 36.

The thinness of the other parts, the violist and violoncellist only plucking their strings, lets the odd palpitation come through.

In the finale are exemplified both the special advantages and the peculiar pitfalls of cyclism. It must be admitted that though the vigor of the original theme is now intensified by the rhythmic squeezing together of three beats into two, there is not quite enough left to say about it, even for an imagination like Brahms's, to hold our interest as closely as the earlier movements do. Of all four movements this is probably the least interesting. Yet the insistent presence of the same character, so to speak, in a different environment, or under a new light, gives it also a fine unity. Thus the second theme, at measure 70, is made of the same notes, F, G, A flat, that at the opening of the movement were so shrill and despairing (first motive of Movement IV, as shown in Figure 33). By simply putting them into a quiet rhythm, and into the key of E flat, so that they get a new relation to the key-note with a far deeper emotional coloring, and letting them expand naturally into a new and broad melody (Figure 36), Brahms gives them a quite new function in the drama, while leaving their identity recognizably the same.

Another subtle example of cyclism is the use made of the "bridge" passage (page 26) with its magnificent sense of momentum in the upper parts, over the sonorous low C of the cello. When it recurs on the last page of all, it is amplified to lead into one final emphatic statement of the main theme of the entire work, in all four instruments. Here it certainly recalls to our subconscious if not to our conscious minds the ending of the first movement. Thus in its close the whole quartet seems to draw itself together for a final enunciation of that note of insatiable will which is the nucleus of its meaning.

CHAPTER X

THE QUARTET IN A MINOR,
OPUS 51, NO. 2

Ask any musician who has played both of the Opus 51 quartets for his opinion of them, and he will be likely to reply that while musically the C minor is unique and cannot be excelled, the A minor "sounds better". To the amateur music-lover this whole matter of "sounding well" is apt to seem a little bewildering. Are music and sound, he will naturally ask, two different things, and is there some basis in reason for the familiar *mot* about Tschaikowsky sounding better than he is, and Brahms not so good? Yes, one must answer, the C minor Quartet is precisely a case in point—a piece that does not always sound as good as it is; in the A minor, on the other hand, music and sound are united in a supreme compatibility.

To make this somewhat baffling point concrete, let us set down in Figure 37 a quotation, in full score, from each quartet. There is no question that the first bit, for all its ingenuity of dovetailing figures, its harmonic and contrapuntal vigor, is apt in performance to verge on the scratchy, while the second, if one may so express oneself, sounds as beautiful as it is. What can be the rationale of such a paradox?

It will be obvious to anyone who ponders the matter that the texture of the string quartet is among the most delicate that music can use; that consequently the art of writing for string quartet involves subtleties seldom to be found in other

music, and requires a supreme skill; and that finally the
amateur listener can hardly hope to understand in detail all the
technical problems a composer must resolve in order to write
a completely successful quartet. *A fortiori* is it obvious how impossible it would be to describe adequately here the complexity
of such problems. Nevertheless, so essential is some sense of

Figure 37.

them to a comprehension of the inner beauties of true string
quartet writing that at least the simpler aspects of the most
important of them must be here briefly discussed.

The music-lover who approaches the string quartet from
the point of view of one who plays the piano hardly realizes
the far-reaching consequences of the simple fact that all his
tones on the piano are ready-made, waiting only for him to
produce them, while every tone that the violinist is to sound he
has first to prepare, by stopping with his left hand the appropriate string *in exactly the right place.* Let his finger, which

often has to be adjusted within the minutest fraction of a second, fall the minutest fraction of an inch too far this way or that, and the tone will be too sharp or too flat. As an inevitable consequence jumps that are perfectly easy on the piano range, for the violin, from difficult, through precarious, to impossible. What is "violinistic" in this regard is precisely the opposite of what is "pianistic." The quick repetitions of one note by viola and cello at the beginning of the C minor Quartet, for example, are admirable for those instruments, enabling them to adjust intonation at the start, and then simply draw the bow easily back and forth. On the piano such repetitions would be uncomfortable: the wrist would tend to stiffen and the tones to become heavy. On the other hand, though it is possible for a violinist to play the filigree passages on page 4 of the same score, he can never play them with as little effort as the pianist who obviously conceived them, since he is obliged to create the intonation of about twelve new notes to each measure. Hence as a general principle, subject of course to all kinds of exceptions, *those figures are most violinistic which involve the least jumping*.

Applying this test now to our quoted passages, we can see that the first is a little unfavorable. The viola and the cello are obliged to make wide jumps, from notes played *staccato* and therefore less secure than if they were bound together, and sometimes "across the strings" (passing from one string to another). Later the violins have to make somewhat similar jumps, thought not in *staccato*. In the second passage, on the contrary, the viola and the second violin have singing melodies that glide along the strings with the utmost advantage of position. Of course this is not to say that passages like the first are not often necessary, nor that the second is musically superior to it; what is meant is simply that the difference between progressing by jumps or quietly along the scale is of great importance to the effects of instruments with fingered strings.

The string quartet contrasts with the piano by another far-reaching technical difference: *it has no pedal sustainment.* The result of this apparently simple fact is that pianists who try to write for string quartet usually find it at first a rather treacherous medium; what sounded so liquid and melting on the piano, thanks to the fusion of the pedal, comes out here dry, hard, and choppy; it is like turning a pastel into a steel engraving. How pathetic in his absurdity is a pianist playing his own quartet (with plenty of pedal) under the illusion that it is going to sound like that! What actually happens on the strings is that only harmonies lasting a certain time build up through their overtones something akin to the fluidity of the pedal; rapidly changing harmonies are always *sec.* We thus discern another superiority, acoustic if not musical, in our second excerpt. In the first the chords change every half measure, sometimes oftener; any sonority that timidly starts up is promptly knocked on the head by the new chord; and the whole is brittle. In the second the harmonies are leisurely, and above all the bass does not change very fast; for virtually two measures it centres on C, and for another two on G. As a result, overtones endue the tonal skeleton with flesh and blood; it no longer rattles like bones, it is soft and yielding, and wears a bloom.

Finally, looking at the whole matter a little more in the large, it is both the limitation and the special glory of the quartet that in mere volume its contrasts must fall far short of those of the orchestra, or even of strings and piano, but that, for this very reason, they are obliged to achieve their artistic aim by far more subtle means. In the orchestra you can oppose a choir of wind or of brass to your strings, or you can divide your many strings into opposing groups, and get a trenchant contrast that will strike the dullest listener. In the quartet you have only four instruments—at every moment of your piece, those four only. No easy mechanical oppositions for the bungler, here. Even if you invent a good contrast, it is no simple matter to tie its two terms together, but requires the most ingenious dovetailing. And your contrasts have all to make up in subtlety what they lack in range. Instead of a trombone against a flute, you have the G-string of the violin against the A of the cello,—or even the D of the violin against its own A,—or even the identical notes in the second violin you have just had in the first. Minute differences of range become crucial; here an instrument has to come forward as leader, there to subordinate itself as second, there again to obliterate itself in useful, necessary accompaniment.

And so we note still a third superiority of our second excerpt, in the precise sense it shows of contrasts so delicate and elusive that only the keenest, most highly trained imagination can use them. For while, in the first, each instrument is well employed, and all produce an effective if hardly a striking texture, in the second each is so peculiarly happy, so "in its element" as we say, that the four together create a unique, a delicious, an unforgettable sound. Viola and second violin carry the melody, in *gemüthlich* thirds and sixths, the viola on top coloring the tune with its individual sober feeling. Cello plucks just the right notes to give the rhythm clearness without obviousness, and to infuse the whole sonority with a delectable lightness. First violin embroiders, touching at crucial points the notes needed as high lights, thus illustrating how even the habitual leader need not always sing, but can be used by a master for purposes of background. And the whole sonority is as individual as it is acoustically faultless.

In the very interest of stating these contrasts there lurks, no doubt, the danger of exaggerating their importance; and it is as well to be on our guard against taking them with a too narrow literalness, and especially against dogmatically translating "different" into "better" and "worse." No doubt the A minor Quartet is more agreeable, in its purely physical sounds, than the C minor; but it would be a sad error to jump from that to the conclusion that it was "better", or that Brahms "ought" to have written the other differently. The two quartets, we might rather say, are different musical beings, and *had* to be differently written. The C minor is far the more profoundly conceived, is more tragic in its feeling, more contrapuntal in its striving melodies, more severe in its search for musical unity; it could not possibly have had the grace, the ease, the charm of the A minor, and yet have remained itself. We do not expect a stormy autumn day, with its heavy clouds allowing only glints of pale sunshine, to woo our senses as Indian summer does with its warm sun and genial air; yet we should not willingly exchange either experience for the other.

In its musical content the A minor Quartet displays the same easy charm as in its tonal setting. Viennese *gemüthlichkeit* is more evident in it than North German earnestness. Yet if it has none of the severe cyclical unity of the other, it achieves an extraordinary unity of its own, through its peculiarly spontaneous yet exact imagination. Indeed its very casualness is a little misleading; we are apt to think that nothing so easy can be remarkable; but the more we study it the more we see that its ease is that of a master diverting himself, and that within its smiling humor a rigorous mind is at work.

Take, for instance, the motive of four notes, the *raison d'être* of the whole movement, which starts off with such disarming naïveté in the first violin: A, F, A, E, a combination of Joachim's *"Frei aber einsam"* with Brahms's own *"Frei aber froh"* motive (or its inversion). For all its apparent casualness, it soon develops most unexpected and entertaining variants.

First, at the end of the exposition, page 6 of the score, it appears in major instead of minor, imitated from second violin to viola, and then to cello. Next, sounded by the cello near the bottom of page 8, it combines with a totally different theme, which we have already heard but at first had supposed to have nothing to do with it, but which now turns out to have been born as a countersubject for it. When, about a page later, the recapitulation begins, we find it altered so as to keep the viola busy with an inversion of the original motive (now F, A, F, B flat). Finally, there exists another kind of imitation of a theme, practiced by the old contrapuntists, in which it is not literally inverted but turned back foremost as if seen in a mirror (as in the scholastic "Spiegel-Canons"). Well, hold page 15 of the score, the coda of the movement, in front of a mirror, and you will see reflected to you the theme, in the second violin thirteen measures from the end, and in the cello four measures later, while it will be visible without mirror in the viola and first violin in adjacent measures. What delectable fooling! . . .

The *Andante moderato* movement is the most serious of the four. Its nobly eloquent theme, with moving bass not only highly characteristic in itself but adding at salient points to the expressiveness of the upper melody (see Figure 38), recalls the exalted mood of that of the *Andante* in the G minor Piano Quartet, but without the false notes in style by which that was marred. Here, so far as style goes, all is Brahms's own. In form it is perhaps not quite so happy, as the middle part, in F sharp minor, in somewhat Hungarian feeling, savors a little of the conventional "contrast", and tends to impair unity. Comparison with such a slow movement as that of the G major Quintet, where all grows out of one theme, will make this clear. Nevertheless it is a fine movement, and its first theme especially is pure Brahms.

The minuet is the first full-fledged example in the chamber music of a new type of light movement to which Brahms at this period was becoming addicted, the essential idea of which is the alternation of lyric with lively sections, unified by some metrical equivalence of beats or measures. In the present instance it is the equal values of their beats that draw together

Figure 38.

the minuet in its languorous grace and the headlong mischievous *Allegretto vivace*. What is boldly and completely different in the two is the building up of their beats into higher organisms. Carried out probably with the unconsciousness of genius, this organization could not have been more systematic had Brahms been consciously putting into practice his knowledge that the most graceful of all rhythms is the triple, the most energetic the duple. In the minuet (see Figure 39, a) all the groupings are by threes. The beat itself is made into an exquisitely graceful triplet by the upper instruments in the second bar, imitated a bar later, with equal grace, by the cello. The beats are themselves grouped in threes, in the aristocratic dignity of the traditional minuet movement. And finally three of these measures, instead of the more usual two or four, are combined to make the phrase: how much of the charm of the whole is due to the three-measure phrases will be realized only gradually.

Figure 39.

Only in the return of the theme in the third "Part" (for the form is three-part also) is the dominance of triple grouping relaxed, and a lovely contrast obtained by the two chords to a beat of the high strings, floating like a captive balloon anchored by the fifths of the cello.

Now turn to the *Allegretto vivace* (Figure 39, b). With the change of mood from grave to gay, everything except the value of the beat changes. The beat is now itself divided into four fleet and coy sixteenth-notes, *staccato*, or a little later into two eighths, not quite so fleet but even more coy. The same energy, acting in wider span, builds the beats into two-beat measures and the measures into two-measure groups, a heavy followed by a light; and even the phrases last usually through four or eight main accents—it is sometimes hard to be sure which. Like a good workman, Brahms is careful to alternate the

Figure 40.

two schemes often enough (even if in the middle he gives us only six measures of the minuet) so that we shall feel, spurred by contrast, the full grace of his threes and the full energy of his twos.

In the finale the Hungarian flavor of the middle part of the slow movement returns. It is a hilarious rondo on two themes. Plastically speaking, its chief interest lies in the imagination with which the czardas-like main theme is varied. In Figure 40 are set down six of the variants, worth our while to savor. In (a) we have the first estate of the theme, headlong but also possessing a certain grace through its three-measure phrasing. At (b) the three-measure phrases are set off by single interpolated measures in which their cadences are playfully imitated; (c) is a vigorous form, with boldly figurated countersubject; (d) is in major, and takes the form of a free canon between cello and first violin; (e) translates the theme, originally so headlong, into ethereal chords that float like clouds on a windless summer day, almost motionless; the passage recalls a memorable, even more beautiful one in Schumann's A minor Quartet. In the last version (f), the final "sprint", the theme is appropriately diminished to two measures. It is hardly necessary to insist on the fertility of thought shown in all these modifications of a single theme. To such mastery the very material of music seems to become fluid.

CHAPTER XI

THE PIANO QUARTET IN C MINOR, OPUS 60

THE third piano quartet is one of the most puzzling problems offered to the student of Brahms's chamber music. Though it was not published until 1875, twelve years after its two companions, it is in many respects less mature than they. Indeed, had we no external evidence about it, internal evidence alone would oblige us to regard it as a curious throw-back, in the work of the forty-year-old Brahms, to a style more youthful than that of his thirties,—a piece of atavism occurring strangely late. Knowing nothing of the history of the score, we should find in it a mixture of styles hard to explain. The very first page, with its Beethoven-like big unisons of the piano (beginning of Figure 41), inaugurating the two chief phrases, and with its later mysterious *pizzicato* E's, followed, as Beethoven might have followed them, by the sudden impetuous downward scale, would take us back to the Brahms of the early orchestral serenades. Then, as we fingered over the score, we should note many other imperfectly assimilated elements of style: the galloping triplets that break into the second theme, and recall the operatic features of the G minor Quartet; the folk-songish sixths so oddly mated with them; the Lisztian bombast of the B major section in the development; the turgid peroration of the movement, in which chamber music style falls victim to piano virtuosity.

In the slow movement, while we should be poor creatures if we let a change of fashion since its day make us indifferent to the real romantic feeling of its song theme (Figure 42), we should none the less feel that the syncopated accompaniment and the cloying chromatics of the cadence savored more of Massenet than of Brahms. The Straussian cadence on its third page would make us smile, but our smile would be only one part amusement to three parts pleasure. The genuine and lovely Brahms of its second theme, *piano, molto dolce*, especially in its heavenly return at the end (Figure 43), would make us supremely happy only for a moment, before the finale came to complete our mystification by its mingling of scholastic counterpoint in the first theme with a chorale for third theme that might have come out of a Tschaikowsky symphony or a Liszt tone-poem, and that touches the false sublime. What, we should ask ourselves, is Brahms, the Brahms who has already achieved the clean distinction of the second Sextet, doing in all these galleys?

In this quandary we should find it helpful to turn for a moment to the scraps of external evidence available. From them we should learn two highly significant facts. First, the C minor Quartet (like the opus 8 Trio, the Piano Quintet, the first Piano Concerto, and the first Symphony) is a work that Brahms kept by him for years, even for decades, and revised over and over again, in a magnificent effort to clarify its original turgidities, to rescue the statue within it, so to speak, from all the superfluous marble that cloaked its outlines. Secondly, he never quite convinced himself that he had succeeded. He treated the piece somewhat as a solicitous parent treats a crippled child. In his insecurely suppressed sense that it was not a complete success he even permitted himself those biographical confidences as to its "meaning", natural enough to more sentimental composers, but always rigorously avoided by him in the case of works sufficiently achieved to speak for themselves.

As early as April, 1854, Brahms brought to Joachim in Hanover the sketch of a piano quartet. It was in C sharp minor, and consisted of an *allegro*, very likely on the themes of the one we now have, a slow movement, probably though not certainly the present one, and a finale, not the one we know. There was no scherzo. The two friends rehearsed it, were dissatisfied with it, and decided that Joachim should keep it by him for further criticism.

In the following autumn, October, 1854, Clara Schumann wrote in her journal: "Brahms has composed a wonderful *Adagio* for his C sharp minor Quartet—full of deep feeling." It is probable though not certain that this movement was essentially the one we know. Quite aside from its key of E major, unusual, however effective, in a quartet in C minor, but very natural if taken over from one in C sharp minor, its whole emotional character suggests the 50's, the *Sturm und Drang* period of the youthful Brahms. We need not necessarily agree with Kalbeck that the quartet reflects Brahms's love for Clara Schumann at the time of Robert Schumann's illness and death; in any case its general tone of youthful feeling is unmistakable. What is more, it is not unlikable, once we associate it with the twenty-year-old youth, even in the sentiment verging on sentimentality of the slow movement. Whatever irreconcilable elements may have later come into the quartet, that one cello theme at least breathes pure boyhood romance, the romance we find in the slow movements of the F minor Piano Sonata and the B major Trio.

Two years later, in November, 1856, Brahms again studied the quartet with his friend Joachim; and again his curious mixture of satisfaction and dissatisfaction with it may be read between the lines of a letter to Clara Schumann: "It seems,"

he writes, "to be very hard to play. Can you study and practice it for some time? Otherwise it will sound abominable. . . ."
Though he kept the quartet by him for over twenty years,
and gave first and last an extraordinary amount of pains
to its revision, the terms in which he refers to it are usually
half serious, half ironical. "Imagine a man," he writes Deiters
in 1868, describing the first movement, "for whom nothing is
left, and who wishes to put an end to himself." In later letters
he makes more precise the association between this music and
the self-destruction of ill-fated lovers by references, couched
in whimsical language in order to disguise the feeling behind
them, to "the man in the blue coat and the yellow waistcoat"
—that is, to Goethe's Werther, type for all Germans of the
unhappy lover. Thus in sending his friend Billroth his manuscript as it exists in 1874, he describes it as "a curiosity—an
illustration for the last chapter in the life of the man in the blue
coat and yellow vest." Even on the verge of publication, in
the autumn of 1875, he writes to his publisher: "On the cover
you must have a picture, a head with a pistol pointed towards
it. Now you can form an idea of the music! For this purpose
I will send you my photograph! Blue coat, yellow breeches and
top-boots would do well, as you seem to like color-printing."

In the summer of 1875 he made radical revisions in preparation for publication. He changed the key from C sharp
minor to C minor, inserted as second movement the present
scherzo, which by its cadence in C major prepares the way for
the slow movement in E major, and replaced the original
finale by a new one. In the fall he was still in his usual divided
mind. "I had a good rehearsal of the Quartet," he writes Simrock, his publisher, "and would have sent it to you the next
day if I had known your (summer) address." Yet he goes on
to say: "the Quartet is half old, half new—the whole thing
isn't worth much!"

If we return now to the internal evidence, to the score itself, we shall be better able to disentangle its contradictory indications. We shall begin to understand why it so oddly weighs down its moments of freshest youthful charm with a monotony of rhythm and a pretentiousness of expression that remind us of the early version of the Opus 8 Trio,—why the really great technical skill it already shows is often not sufficient to make truly memorable the musical thoughts it can manoeuvre, but cannot lift above academic routine. This is particularly evident in the scherzo and the finale, the two dullest movements. The scherzo theme, despite some fine suspensions, has a busy, braggadocio air conventional compared to the originality of the G minor Quartet intermezzo or the scherzo of the Piano Quintet. The theme of its trio is a bit of scholastic counterpoint, close cousin to the "scrap-basket theme" of the A major Quartet scherzo. In the finale the only particularly individual theme is the chorale; and that, alas, seems from the start less a sincere expression than a "plant," put in with an eye to effective peroration. We are scarcely surprised, only sorry, when in the coda, which for once falls below rather than rising above the rest of the piece, the piano tears it to shreds, while the strings interject their increasingly frequent triplets "as per specifications"; and we realize that this is orchestral or operatic music, only masquerading as a quartet.

Even the first movement does not entirely escape the same faults. Its general tone is the same melodramatic one we find in the first version of the B major Trio, often verging, especially in the coda, on turgidity. What is even more serious, its themes, again like those of the early trio, lack salient rhythmic contrast, and show little of the magnificent dynamic capacity to evolve that we associate with the mature Brahms. They are shown in Figure 41; and while the second has charm, and rivals those of the slow movement in its power to haunt our memories, it is thetic like the first. Both are thus too similar for either to stand out strongly. The result is that in the sequel neither takes the reins into its own hands, and goes

Figure 41.

Theme 1.

Theme II.

rejoicing on its inevitable way; the composer has to stand constantly behind them with whip, spur, or goad.

On the other hand, even with this material, which one fancies the Brahms of the 70's took over from the 50's largely through motives of sentiment, his maturing technique in composition suffices to achieve some splendid moments. Whereve the themes recreate themselves in his later manner we fee a new power carrying them forward. Such a place is the quie beginning of the development, with its kaleidoscopic regrouping of harmonies. Such another is the very end of the coda, where

Figure 42.

after the turmoil dies away, the gentle conclusion theme first heard at the end of the exposition, in E flat, is modified to bring a noble if gloomy cadence in somberest C minor.

But the real heart of the C minor Quartet is of course the slow movement—that lovely outpouring of youthful sentiment so naïve and so full-throated that we almost welcome its traces of sentimentality as vouching its untouched genuineness. Its second theme, quite free from the over-ripeness of the first, slender and wistful as youth, is the high point of the whole work. Those lovely hesitant chromatics in the violin, at the

bottom of page 36, so delicately relieved against the clear
treble triplets of the piano—the continuation where against

Figure 43.

the wide deliberate arpeggios of the piano the strings sigh their
unanswered questions—and then the return, in softest treble
sonorities, with no bass but the viola—all this is the unique,
the incomparable Brahms, the Brahms that, whether in the

slow movement of the first trio or the variations of the last
clarinet sonata, seems timeless and perfect. The last page
of this movement, where the same hesitantly questioning theme
coupled now with the opening notes of the cello's song, take
leave of us, is one of the most individual pages in the entire
chamber music.

One can understand that the mind capable of achieving
such a miracle of beauty as this could not but be a severe critic
of its own less inspired imaginings. One almost wonders
whether, blowing hot and cold as Brahms did about this quartet
through two decades, he did not finally save it for this one
page. Probably not; and certainly it has manifold other interests for the student of his works. Tireless revision, the
artist's virtue, cannot, any more than any other virtue, always
triumph. . . . The C minor Quartet may stand in our mind
as in large part one of those noble failures that underlie and
prepare, as all good workmen know, the successes which alone
the naïve public acclaims.

CHAPTER XII

THE QUARTET IN B FLAT, OPUS 67

I F the C minor String Quartet might be briefly described as
that of drama, and the A minor as that of sentiment, the B flat
would undoubtedly have to be set down as the quartet of humor. And since probably for every hundred people who re-
spond to drama, and for every thousand who appreciate sentiment, there are hardly ten who either are sensitive to humor or
have any wish to be, we shall not be surprised that the last
quartet is the least popular of the three. Adolfo Betti tells how
he once heard it performed by the Joachim Quartet, in Brahms's
presence. Despite its beauty, there was little applause.

Humor, suggests Overstreet in an enlightening analysis,[1]
is the product of a sort of playfulness or irresponsibility. It en-
visages incongruities without the disapproval of common sense
and adult wisdom, with an almost childlike pleasure and sympathy; free from self-importance, and able to inhibit its sense
of practicality, it throws itself with zest into the play of oppositions, of contradictions, even of absurdities. This requires
high spirits and a kind of youthfulness; and the reason we all
so deeply resent being denied the possession of humor, as
Overstreet also shows, is that we are thus by implication denied
also youth and gusto. Most of us, however, even those whose
humor serves them well in other spheres, consider it out of
place in our dealings with music. Music, we suppose, is at home
with passion, with romance, with sentiment, but can never

[1] *Influencing Human Behavior*, by Harry A. Overstreet.

117

descend from the sublime to the ridiculous. Look at us as we
sit bolt upright in the concert hall or the chamber music drawing room, and you will see that we have laid our sense of humor
safely on the shelf before we started in to listen to music.

Not only is the exercise of humor in music frowned upon
by convention; it is also with difficulty comprehensible to reason. We can understand how words, with their definite references to external facts, can suggest the incongruous, but it is
hard to see how such incongruity can extend to tones, which
correspond to nothing in the extra-musical world. Consequently
when Arthur Whiting tells us, for example, that most people's
idea of patriotism is expressed in the formula "God bless our
'tis of thee," we smile, because we recognize the two halves of
the sentence, and also recognize that the two things they refer
to do not belong together. But how, we ask, could music do
anything like that?

Nevertheless music is full of just such delightful incongruities; and if we do not smile at them it is because we are
either too solemnly self-important, too relentlessly bent on
"culture" to allow ourselves such relaxation, or else—and this
is perhaps oftener the case—not sufficiently familiar, through
years of attentive experience of music, with its more intangible
implications, to be amused when these are confused and contra-
dicted. The unexpected can of course be savorsome only to those
who have expectations. Only if we have acquired definite musical
habits do we smile when Mozart begins the trio of the minuet
of his Jupiter Symphony with the formula of the complete
dominant-tonic cadence with which it is customary to end a
phrase, and closes his phrase with the kind of running melody
that sounds more like an opening: we smile, because our musical
habits are being piquantly snubbed. We perceive an incongruity quite comparable to that of beginning a sentence with
the perfectly good beginning "God bless our," and ending it

with the perfectly good ending " 'tis of thee"—when this perfectly good beginning and ending just do not happen to fit. Naturally, however, such incongruity seems such only to those listeners who have formed habits of expecting the congruous; and for the formation of such habits many music-lovers are too inexperienced or too inattentive. Hence humor is of all musical qualities the least appreciated.

In his delightful analysis Overstreet, braving the contempt reserved for those who attempt to explain the sense of humor, shows not only what it is, but how its aëration of the mind may be encouraged. Taking a leaf from his book, we may ask ourselves both how humor may inspire a composer, and how we as listeners may fit ourselves to follow him in his enjoyment of its peculiar savor. We shall find that while it always takes for granted the associations of normal musical experience, it also takes an irresponsible delight in following these associations through unexpected and unconventional paths, in generally turning everything upside down and topsy-turvy, and making us expect one thing only in order to give us something quite different—and much more piquant! Its spirit is a sort of reasonable irrationality, logical nonsequaciousness, solemn mischief, highly puzzling to the literal, and heady as wine. Like the young man in Stevenson's "The Wrong Box" who interchanged all the labels in the luggage-van and sent all the packages to people for whom they were not intended, it combines with an exact sense of the value of labels a naughty-boyish enjoyment in their confusion. It follows out its associations, never with the predetermined and dull automatism of convention, but with a delicious haphazardness, an inspired irrelevance.

When music is written in this spirit, only the listener who approaches it in the same spirit can really understand and enjoy it; the merely routine listener will find himself completely at sea. In order therefore to enjoy the Brahms B flat Quartet, we shall do well to invoke Meredith's spirit of comedy. For when Brahms begins with a horn salvo in triplets (Figure 44, a)

Figure 44.

* *Thematic II Violin part.*

which, with its *forte* repetitions by all four instruments of the *piano* fanfares proposed by the middle two, seems as straightforward, as bent on business, as any self-respecting horn salvo ought to be, your conventional listener is at once cajoled into feeling that if there is one thing that that salvo can be relied upon to do, it is to keep up the even flow of eighth-notes its opening seems so reassuringly to guarantee. Yet, before a page is out, it is being nefariously held up at every third note (Figure 44, b). Again, the motives of its first two measures are essentially opening motives; their connotation, thanks in part to the *staccato* and to the accents, is of the vigor of starting. Nevertheless it is precisely these motives which, quieted by being played *legato,* and artfully transplanted to the closing measures of the phrase, are used in the second theme (Figure 44, c) to form not its opening but its cadence. In other words, Brahms is here reversing Mozart's little jest of beginning with a cadence, in such a way as to make a cadence out of a beginning—and what a fresh one!

Thus far he has almost pointedly avoided the key-note; its avoidance keeps the music always on the move; even this odd cadence of the second theme reaches not the key-note but only the third step, much less decisive. This same bit now, however, as if on a sudden happy impulse, turns from major to minor, and from the cosiness of harmony to the hollow mysteriousness of two-part writing, widely spaced (Figure 45, a), and soon slides demurely but decisively down to the key-note, F. And with that, as if such a home-coming could not be left unfêted, the time changes to 2–4, and in a new and saucy rhythm the music kicks up its heels and proceeds to play with that F as a cat with a mouse that has not been too easy to catch. (Figure 45, b.) And all this, we must remember, in the sonata-form of the traditional first movement,—but surely a sonata-form of a casualness, of a seemingly almost accidental improvisation, such as only a madcap fancy could contrive.

It is worth while to observe that even Brahms, boldly inventive as he is of rhythmic transformations of this kind in his lighter movements, here tries for the first time applying them to a sonata-form. The two- and four-fold division of the beat in the conclusion theme (only the start of which is shown in Figure 45, b) are saliently contrasted with the triplets of the opening horn salvo, while unity is assured by the retention of the strict values of the beat itself. In the course of the develop-

Figure 45.

ment Brahms takes occasion to combine and recombine these contrasting rhythms in all sorts of whimsical ways, keeping us, as we say, "guessing"; and even more putting us on tenter-hooks by a great many "empty first beats" (as at the start of the development) which prolong our doubts as to which of several possible rhythms is to follow. And in the coda he throws all his aces on the table in one generous handful, and we are regaled by "empty firsts," by threes against fours, and even by threes to a measure, in a perfect harlequinade of fun.

The *Andante* strikes us at first, possibly, as less individual than the first movement. Its melody is rather Mendelssohnian, while the syncopated chords of the accompaniment seem some-what pianistic and Schumannesque. There is also, if we compare its type of construction with that of the *Andante* of the A minor Quartet, the suggestion of a tendency to stereotype. Here as there we find a broad theme building up Parts I and III of a three-part form, with between them a middle part that, as the wag said, "seems to be there because there has to be a middle part, rather than because that middle part has to be." But the beauty of the main theme saves the day. Very fine is the dignity of its opening phrases; beautiful is the touch of sombre A flat major with which its F major is darkened in the contrast-section; powerful, at the return, is the march of the cello down an octave to its low C, by scale steps the evenness and inevitability of which are deeply stirring. And we are made to forget the perfunctoriness of the middle part by the charm with which the main theme, when it recurs in D major, is parcelled out between changing groups of instruments.

Extraordinary are both the color and the expression of the elusive *Agitato* (*Allegretto non troppo*), which serves as a scherzo, and in which the viola takes the lead throughout, its hoarse voice almost rasping against the suppressed tones of the other three instruments, played with mutes. The contrast of muted and non-muted tone is highly original. How beautiful is the coloring, for instance, at the repetition of the theme, when the muted first violin adds a delicate silver edge, so to speak, to the dark, tormented, almost agonized cries of the viola! Towards the middle there are fascinating confrontations of simple triads, so placed that incompatible notes color successive chords in most contradictory ways, and the ear is kept on the alert to catch the kaleidoscopically changing flavors. The return of the theme is lengthily and subtly prepared. Less striking is the trio, purposely:—a sort of neutral moment of rest from the exquisite, almost painful beauty of the other. . . . As a whole, this irresistible intermezzo is of a kind of which Brahms alone seems to possess the secret. Its shy hesitations, its wayward fancies, its moments of frank headlong sentiment, above all its sustained atmosphere of a kind of strained, agonized, breathless loveliness, combine into an unique whole, and when with a whiff of D major and a blur of dissonance between the pedal D's of first violin and cello it flickers out, we feel that we have seen for a moment Beauty herself.

Figure 46.

The ingenious use of cyclism made at the end of the finale, though it may remind us of that supreme stroke at the end of the Third Symphony, is here made in its own terms, and to a unique consummation. What strikes us first in the finale, which begins as a set of variations, is the humor and charm of its theme. Conceived in folk vein with its naïve repeated F's, it is shaped in familiar three-part form, but with several happy idiosyncrasies which delight us ever more as they keep returning in the variations. Its sixteenth-note anacruses, very important in unifying it, are managed deftly so that their climactic order impresses us from the start: the first begins on low D, the second on high D, the third on high G. The cadence of the first four-measure phrase (Part I of the highly concise form) is also striking—a sudden evasion of the key of B flat at the last moment, to land in the much brighter, more ethereal key of D major. This Part is repeated.

Short as is the contrast of Part II—only another four measures—it has room for a number of *trouvailles*. It swells up to the high F sharp in such a way that the thetic rhythm (accenting the F sharp) and the dissonant harmony of this motive F sharp, E, B flat, make it stand out strongly as the climax of this Part. It is artfully shaped, however, as an augmentation of the motive in the opening phrase beginning with an anacrusis on D. The result is that Brahms can use it as a preparation for returning, through two other anacrustic appearances of the same motive, descending in pitch and in loudness, to his theme, which recurs at the ninth measure with deeply satisfying inevitability.

But in this return comes the real "find." For the best surprise of all is when Brahms, having given us the two opening measures of his theme again, and having thus got our mouths fairly open for the last two, suddenly says to us debonairly: "That's all! You thought you were going to have a cadence, didn't you? Well, I've shown you in the first movement how a cadence can be made out of an opening, and this opening is all the cadence you are going to get, so you may as well enjoy it." And then, to make sure we take his point, he repeats the whole six measures of contrast and return, and we are obliged to recognize those two measures of truncated return as start and finish all rolled into one by the condensing power of his wit.

Through six variations the theme is discussed by the four friends, the viola at first acting informally as chairman and toastmaster, the violin gradually reasserting his natural leadership. With the fifth variation the tonality moves to D flat major, and in the next to the still darker G flat major. By this time the theme has, as it were, evanesced and been dissipated into air; all that remains of it, under the poising chords, is its ghost plucked by cello and viola . . . A pause. . . . And then, by a sudden swoop of the violin, we are brought back, all at once, to B flat major, to daylight and to—no, not to the variation theme, but by the cyclical scheme which Brahms has had up his sleeve all the time, to the horn salvo theme from the first movement—that is, to the main theme of the whole quartet. But—and here is the peculiarity of this special application of cyclism—in this seventh variation, which is treated more broadly and freely than the others, the first movement theme is only for the melodic figuration, and the variation theme, though not bodily present, is still kept also in our consciousness by its characteristic modulation to D major. It is as if, as Kalbeck prettily says, the two themes here "took leave of each other, like lovers." Yet they do not really, after all, take leave of each other, or if so only like lovers in light opera, for although from this point on the hero of the quartet as a whole more and more asserts his cyclical priority, the more feminine variation theme is by no means disposed to leave him the field. Even the second theme of the first movement, too, has its moment of importance, through page 37. Then, through the last three pages, we have most plentiful and unforeseen combinations of the triplet motive of the horn salvo with the naïve anacruses and repeated notes of the variation theme, until at last, in the closing dozen measures, they join hands, come down-stage, and wave kisses to us, as they are finally hidden by a "quick curtain." . . . And so this charming comedy that Brahms has made his themes enact for our benefit closes with just the right touch of operetta.

III

MASTERSHIP

FACSIMILE OF A PAGE OF SKETCHES FOR THE CLARINET SONATA IN F MINOR

(Courtesy of the *Gesellschaft der Musikfreunde*, Vienna.)

Very few sketches of Brahms survive. The sheet in the possession of the *Gesellschaft der Musikfreunde* is written half in ink, half in pencil; and the whole is stricken through with rough pencil lines. The ink half outlines sixty-seven measures of the opening *Allegro*, showing the essential motives of the first and second themes. The pencil portion shows the first eight-bar period of the theme of the *Allegretto*, the third movement, with four more bars of the clarinet figuration, and the entire twelve bars of the middle part. The whole is written at breakneck speed. There are few if any significant changes, such as might give us some insight into the composer's mental processes. The ink extensions of certain bar-lines upward, however, are of great interest as showing how conscious he was of the uneven rhythmic divisions which gave his music such flexibility: for example, at the very start these projections show the four-bar group of the piano followed and completed by the seven-bar group of the clarinet. Also of interest, in view of Brahms's predilection for rhythmic augmentations "across the bar," is his shorthand method of writing the last two bars in the sketch as one.

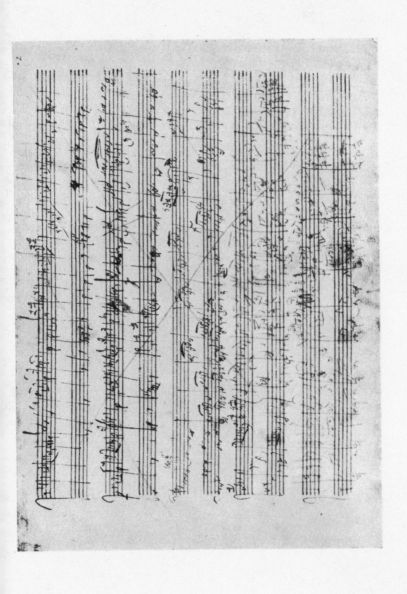

CHAPTER XIII

THE VIOLIN SONATA IN G MAJOR, OPUS 78

THE twelve works extending from Brahms's first violin sonata, written in 1879, after three previous sonatas had been lost or destroyed by him, to the clarinet sonatas which complete the list, exemplify his completest mastery. Only in the last four does any falling off in freshness of inspiration become perceptible. In all the others sentiment and skill are at last in perfect balance, the forces of growth and of decay reach for the brief moment of prime their precarious equilibrium. Here he comes as near perfection as human limitations permit.

Never had he imagined a lovelier bit of melody than the opening theme, with its gentle insistence on the thrice-repeated D which as "motto" repeated cyclically in all three movements dominates the whole sonata, and its equally gentle fall, more tender than melancholy, to the lower D. The essential features of this theme have been transcribed for piano in Figure 47. It will be noticed that the "three-note motive," after its octave fall, is followed by a rising motive of reviving energy, as characteristic as the other in outline, and indeed beginning with the same threefold repetition of a single note. Still another motive, a vigorous dip and rise, first heard in the fifth measure, completes the theme, every particle of which is thus significant.

If we wish fully to savor the innocent, placid character of this theme, we shall do well to remark two of its peculiarities, one rhythmic, one tonal. The rhythmic one is that all three

of its motives, different as they are in other respects, begin
with "empty first beats," the first even prolonging this pause
through four beats.   Hence a marked hesitation, to which the
tune owes much of its expression of gentle quietude.   This is
enhanced by the second, tonal peculiarity that, as in so many

Figure 47.

of Brahms's melodies, all its main tones are taken out of the
simplest central chords of the key: the tonic in the first two
measures, the subdominant in the third, the tonic again in the
fourth.   The freedom from dissonance, the perfectly forthright
movement through the chord, gives an equability of sentiment
that exactly matches the rhythmic ease and deliberation.   Before we go any further let us clinch these impressions by contrasting the form of the same theme that comes after the musical drama has generated some heat, and that is shown in
Figure 48.   Already, we see, the theme has lost innocence—and
acquired intensity.   If we ask ourselves how, we observe that

he "empty firsts" have been exchanged for anacruses of the
irst two repeated notes, launching the theme on the third as
a strong thesis, while the consonant harmonies have at the same
ime given place to dissonant ones, to which many suspended
iotes impart tension. This is a good example of the subtlety
of the means of expression the mature Brahms has at his
command.

Figure 48.

It is interesting to compare these two forms of the theme
with two others. Look first at the resumption of the theme by
he violin at the anacrusis to the twenty-first measure, answered in that measure by the piano. Imitations between the
instruments now transform what began as a monologue into
a lively dialogue, so that the theme almost forgets its in-
iocence, and takes on a new emphasis. The violin begins with
he anacrustic form, to which the piano answers with the empty-
beat form. As the violin proceeds with the original melody in
measure 23 the piano begins to imitate itself, in more lively
rhythms and with changing harmonies. By measure 25, the
hird and boldest of the original motives becomes matter for
ively give-and-take, soon accelerating to quick-fire imitations
of its first two notes only, dovetailing ingeniously between the

violin and the piano. By this packing closer and closer of the imitations, the composer excites our emotions at the same time that he delights our intelligence.

The other passage just reverses the methods of this one; beginning at the *In tempo, poco a poco e crescendo* twenty-one measures from the end, it is the broadening and simplification of the theme needed to quiet it as it prepares for the close. Note that the harmonies now change more slowly, each lasting a measure. Note the tranquil, even progress of *legato* quarter-notes in the new continuation of the melody. Above all, note the novel rhythmic grouping the composer here for the first time gives to the chief motive: by starting the three D's on the second instead of the fifth beat (thus using only one empty beat instead of four) he gives to the third D, the most important note of all, a longer duration than it has yet had, thus making it more lingering and expressive. After the quiet passage here shown, a few brilliant evolutions quickly bring the movement to an end.

The slow movement is based on a broad theme in E flat major, given out by the piano alone. While the opening motive of six notes is of an expression earnestly serious, becoming towards the end of the movement nobly impassioned, a suggestion of pastoral innocence and peace is given by the horn calls that immediately follow it—and this element too reaches an apotheosis in the closing measures of the movement.

With the indication *più andante* comes a striking change of mood. The sustained singing style of the *Adagio* theme is interrupted by a strange heaving movement in the bass, punctuated by silences that almost gasp, and rising from restless foreboding to passionate insistence, while all the time sombre chords above it harp on the three reiterated notes of the cyclic motive, given now a dark and fatalistic coloring. This motive, though here much more subordinate than in the first and last movements, lends an irresistible forward propulsion to the *più andante* section. As the violin takes up in turn its gasping, laboring phrases, the piano bass follows in imitation, increasing the tension through a passage of highly complex rhythmic involution until, with the same passage imitated from the piano bass to the violin, the motive resolves itself into hammer-strokes by which both instruments fight their way to the dominant chord of D minor which caps the climax.

Then comes a curious transformation. The three rising notes into which the original cyclic motive has been shaping itself, losing now their boldness and taking on a shy timidity, begin to rise in soft, hesitant imitation through several registers of the piano. As they approach their higher limit the violin, with equal hesitance, suggests the opening notes of the *Adagio* theme, changed tonally and rhythmically to only the ghost of itself. The piano quietly moves up a little, and repeats its timid ladder of motives. A little more confidently the violin insists on the *Adagio* theme. Again the piano moves up, and now both instruments pause as if contemplating that other theme. Shall they embark upon it again? Shall they leave the passion of the *più andante* behind, and launch themselves on the quieter, deeper waves of the *Adagio*, and of the rich key of E flat major? . . . It is one of Brahms's most finely conceived "preparations," leading us so gently yet so firmly up to the very brink of the returning theme.

The first part is now repeated, with richer ornamentation than at first, and cadencing into a coda where the uneasy bass of the *più andante* returns in a chastened and still more sombre mood. The violin now soars like a hawk on a summer afternoon, with outspread wings, scarcely moving. But as the bass motive, succumbing to this languor, seems about to stop entirely, and sinks to D flat, the violin, reawakening, brings the first phrase of the theme, in eloquent double-stops, in the rich key of G flat. This reëntrance of the theme, at the twelfth measure from the end, is the signal for a free and poignant treatment of its motive, echoed from violin to piano, reduced to its three most vital notes, too eager to wait for the bar-lines but falling on whatever beat happens to lie near, and through these serrated rhythms rising at last to fierce insistence, at the *forte* where both instruments declaim it together. With that the passion dies away, and the horn calls return, in lovely relenting of mood, flowering into gracious piano arabesques to which the violin responds with a simplicity more ineffable than any elaboration.

In a work so highly organized as this sonata, a work in which a single root motive reappears in each movement, and the last pages gather together all the threads and reconcile all the moods, it need not surprise us to find the composer working backward from his conclusion to his premises, and to discover not in the opening movement but in the closing one the key to the whole. This key is the threefold repetition of a single note we have already encountered so often—but as it appears neither in the first nor the second movements, but in the finale, and in the two songs, "Regenlied" and "Nachklang," written in the summer of 1873, six years before the sonata, from which it was borrowed for the finale.

If we reduce the songs, both of which are written in F sharp minor and in *Alla breve*, two half-notes to the measure, to the key and time-measure of the finale (G minor, four quarters) we find that its first two measures come directly from them. The following measures, on the other hand, depart from them in a way no less interesting, and highly instructive as to a master's methods of composition. In the first two measures of Figure 49, the poetic suggestion from the rainy day is clear in the intimate quietude that the first two D's take on from their position as a gentle anacrusis in the violin (frequently echoed in the piano) and more literally in the lapping sixteenth-note figure of the accompaniment, maintained through a large part

Figure 49.

"Rain Theme"

Cadence in "Regenlied:"

of the movement. It will be noted, however, that the cadence on the dominant of the following two measures differs from that of the "Regenlied" (and of "Nachklang" as well), which is shown at the end of the figure, and which is on the sub-mediant, E flat.

Now it is certainly curious that in this masterly finale to a sonata written in 1879 we find the theme of the songs written six years earlier occurring in three refrains, but *with its original cadence only in the third and last refrain.* In the first two refrains Brahms substitutes the new melodic outline and the dominant cadence shown in the figure. In other words, here is a composer who, after he has had a melody in his head for six years, has enough command of his own thoughts and enough understanding of composition to withhold its original form through eight pages, and use it on the ninth! We have seen in the case of the motive of the first movement what extraordinary flexibility of manipulation Brahms had at his command —how he could give one theme, by simple but far-reaching harmonic and rhythmic changes, many entirely different shades of expression. Obviously, the present instance is only a more striking one of the same essential procedure. Once we have heard the dominant cadence, and felt its superior tranquillity to that of the stronger cadence to the sub-mediant, we cannot but recognize how right Brahms was to adopt it, how preferable it is for all that early part of the movement picturing the serene intimateness of the rainy day. It is only on its last appearance that the theme needs to move a little more assertively; even then any change more violent than this one to the sub-mediant would tend to disrupt so delicate a fabric.

At about the middle of the movement, after the rain-theme refrain has been twice heard in its entirety, the key changes to that of the *Adagio,* E flat, and the violin, in double-stops all the more soulful by contrast with the light texture of what has gone before, sings the opening motive of the slow movement. Almost without waiting for its completion, the piano begins to vary the horn call which originally followed it by turning it into the sixteenth-notes of the lapping rain-drops (See Figure 50, a). Thus are the first two motives only of this theme, formerly so broad and singing, detached from it, and made gradually to take on the character of the rainy day. Imperceptibly they lose their sustained flow, they become just a part

Figure 50.

of the ubiquitous dripping and pattering (Figure 50, b). Thus for the moment the *Adagio* theme is only suggested, is subdued, so to speak, to its new environment, and presently gives way entirely to the third, last, and more agitated refrain of the rain-theme.

But as this draws again to a close, the lapping piano figures rise in an arpeggio that is now at last in major, and this brighter

G major supplants the long gray G minor as gradually as the sun burns away a mist, shining abroad at first palely and then with increasing warmth. In this new G major atmosphere the *Adagio* theme returns once more in the piano, while simultaneously the lapping figures sound above it in the violin, not to be withheld. Everything seems at once to brighten and to

Figure 51

soften, and the lapping version of the horn call supports in the piano (Figure 50, c) a tender violin phrase that might come from either theme, so fully are they now coalesced.

And then, in the last six measures (Figure 51) the thrice-repeated note of the whole sonata is heard for the last time, rising to higher and higher pitch, with tenderer and tenderer resolutions, alternately in the two instruments. As the violin reaches and poises upon the high D, the piano, its left-hand part finishing the lapping rain-figure, remembers in the upper register two notes of the horn call, now become A and G, and weaves them into a final tender curve of cadence. At the same time the violin expands the four equal notes from the first measure of the theme, now clear and confident in major, in an ecstatic augmentation. The long subdominant cedes at last to the tonic; and the music sinks to complete rest, to perfect peace . . . and to silence.

CHAPTER XIV

THE C MAJOR TRIO, OPUS 87

As a concrete instance of the difference between the youthful fancy and the manly imagination of a man of genius, contrast the opening of the C major Trio with that of any of the early works. Here, in the first theme transcribed for piano in Figure 52, all is as rigorous, as free of surplusage, as direct and inevitable, as a mathematical equation. Grant the premise posed in the first four measures, and the rest must follow. The theme rises irresistibly from C through E to F, and then to G, all in a characteristic rhythm. Then, when the piano enters, with a downward octave jump that answers the upward jump of the strings by inversion (a device steadily dearer to Brahms from this period on), the strings still maintain their upward struggle, through A, B, D, and finally up to the high F, before the first breathing-space is reached. Note all through here the spareness of the writing, its athletic muscularity, free from any adipose tissue: how for instance the piano part contains practically nothing but those octave jumps, in contrary motion in the two hands, and crowding in their excitement into Brahms's favorite shifted rhythms. In the thirteenth measure cello and violin bring forward the first two of the many ingenious variants of the opening motive which multiply as the movement proceeds; and by the twenty-first measure, where our figure ends, Brahms has made more of his theme than he was able to make even of a motive so interesting as that of the G minor Quartet in the whole exposition.

The same closely packed texture, made possible by his supreme mastery of counterpoint, enables him to say all he needs
to say for the moment about his contrasting motive of three

Figure 52.

quarter-notes (immediately diminished to three eighth-notes,
asymmetrically placed in the measure) within the twelve bars
that lead up to the return of the main theme. In this return also
the closeness of texture is extraordinary—the theme in octaves

in the strings, and simultaneously in two other, different rhythms in the piano, and the continuation made from new combinations of the octave jumps. The last drop of meaning is squeezed from the D reached as apex by the two strings, and from its stout resistance to the piano harmonies that assault it (in the octave-jump figure) and that finally compel it to descend to C, which in turn resists through ten more abating measures.

Only with the entrance of the lyrical second theme does the tension relax. The three quarter-notes of the earlier contrast section, there so passionately restless, here lose their anacrustic momentum and their troubled tonal intervals, and become tranquil, almost suave, in a thetic rhythm and a gentle melodic inflection. The lightly fanciful descending triplets which presently provide contrast seem at first equally relaxed; but they soon lead to a restlessly rhythmed form of the same three notes, *forte*, in a sort of jerky triplet, which affords the only other moment of stress before the easy-going *grazioso* tune that closes the statement of themes.

The development begins with the main theme, in passionate, phantasmagoric struggles. But presently, with the deceptive cadence to D flat major, and the indication *Animato*, comes calm, and a wondrous new variant of the same Protean theme. Its rhythm expanded by augmentation, its whole atmosphere warmed and enriched by the change of key, it becomes a noble, poising melody, deliberately sung, first by cello, and then, in C sharp minor, by violin. The high continuity of it all is due not only to the constant Brahmsian renewal of melody by which each goal reached becomes a new starting point, but also to the masterly use of dissonances to suspend the sense. In her account of her lessons with Brahms, Florence May says: "He loved Bach's suspensions. 'It is here that it must sound,' he would say, pointing to the tied note, and insisting, whilst not

allowing me to force the preparation, that the latter should be so struck as to give the fullest possible effect to the dissonance."
. . . From this point to that at which the development merges into the recapitulation as a cataract foams into a rushing river, the stormy mood returns and grows ever stormier, and the various motives swirl together ever more phantasmagorically. Just as the mind begins to grow dizzy, they straighten out into a broad unison of the second and third measures of the theme, and the theme itself returns in a form intensified by more motion and by the heightened harmony. The recapitulation repeats the essential features of the exposition unchanged, and there is a magnificently concentrated coda.

The *Andante con moto* is a set of variations on a theme of highly original emotion and coloring, carried out with a technical mastery that we appreciate but gradually, as careful study makes it familiar. What we naturally and rightly feel most strongly at first is the peculiarly individual emotional tone of this music—the same melancholy earnestness, at once stoic and passionate, that breathes from such later Brahmsian works as the "Four Serious Songs." The theme itself, with its hollow minor mode, its weary rise from the keynote and sad return to it, and its further even wearier and sadder descent to the dominant note E, strikingly recalls the refrain of the D minor song, the burden of the grievous meditation: "That which befalleth the sons of men befalleth beasts; even one thing befalleth them; as the one dieth, so dieth the other," with the solemn conclusion, "Wherefore I perceive that there is nothing better than that a man should rejoice in his own works; for that is his portion."

And just as in the song one is steadily conscious of a pulsing power beneath the bare, severely restrained phrases, so that their final effect is no less impassioned than austere, so in this theme the phrases follow each other with a powerful and passionate logic. Emotional impulse and technical invention are here working in such complete unanimity that the strict structural system which appears in the theme and is rigorously preserved in every minor variation—and in its essentials in the major variation also—is but the outer expression of an equally strict spiritual truth. The essential lines of this splendid theme have been transcribed for piano in Figure 53.

The first two phrases, up to the double bar, state the fundamental musical thought in severe plainness. In the third phrase the very weight and sad earnestness of the music carry it naturally down to the subdominant, D minor. The balance is redressed by a return to the tonic, A minor, in the fourth phrase, which might be the last, did not the impatience by which the melody begins to anticipate each of its phrases show us how much latent feeling is hidden under the grave accents of the earlier phrases, that must now come out. Sure enough, in the fifth and sixth phrases, the increasing emotional intensity not only cuts the rhythms in half but forces modulations, logical but bold, into D and even into E, and carries the tune finally up to the high F, further intensified by a *sforzando* and by an eloquent grace-note. This is the acme of the climax. With phrases seven and eight come the descending curve and the quieting emotion. They seek the central tonic A again, and by an overlapping of rhythms that makes the closing measure of the first identical with the opening measure of the second, the final character of that A chord is emphasized. It is interesting to note that all the variations follow the theme literally in the tonal rise and rhythmic shortening of the more intense phrases, and all but the last follow it in the overlapping of the conclusive ones; the last naturally expands these a little.

More than this, there is a strict and peculiar reciprocal relation between these two final phrases, followed also in all the variations in minor, though not in the major one, that il-

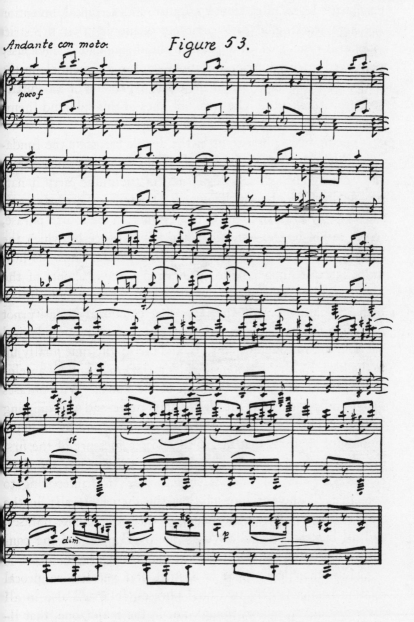

Andante con moto. Figure 53.

lustrates strikingly the emotional value that contrapuntal devices came to have for the later Brahms. Phrase 8, in the
theme and in all the variations except the fourth, is a litera
(and of course increasingly complex) *Inversion* of Phrase 7
The two closing phrases are thus given a sort of monumental

Figure 54.

Closing two phrases of the Variations in minor.

schematic beauty. As we listen attentively to them, as they
take shape in the theme, we feel not only an intellectual and aes-
thetic satisfaction in their exact balance, but an emotional truth
that is peculiar to this kind of strict inversion: the buoyant accents of the violin find their necessary complement and echo
in the sad but noble tones of the cello, and its final rise to the E
is as questioning, as uncertain and troubled, as the fall of the

violin to A is assured and confident. Emotion has its logic as well as reason. In Figure 54 are set down, in melodic outline only, these closing phrases of the first three variations, becoming as they proceed, it will be noticed, not only more complex

Figure 55.

Closing phrases of the last variation

structure but more moving in expression. Figure 55 shows the corresponding phrases of the last variation, and in fuller texture the natural extension that closes the movement. Seldom has even Brahms conceived a more exquisite rhythmic augmentation than that at the very end, in the 9–8 measure that substitutes three beats for two as if giving the music a moment to hold its breath before uttering the tender final notes.

After an agreeably light-footed scherzo of the *misterioso* type we reach a finale worthy by its conciseness to companion the first two movements, but inferior to them in material. For the theme as a melody we acquire a belated toleration only when, in the coda, it is treated by augmentation just as was that of the first movement. From that point on, the interest so increases that a movement which began by being only "jolly" ends by becoming high-spirited.

CHAPTER XV

THE VIOLA QUINTET IN F MAJOR, OPUS 88

In his two viola quintets, so called because in them he adds a second viola to the traditional string quartet, Brahms returns to a type of concerted music he had practiced with so much success in his two early sextets. It was a type peculiarly congenial to him, permitting that close-packed fulness of sound to which his romantic side inclined him, yet exacting too the vigorous workmanship in which his contrapuntal skill delighted to exercise itself. The cleanness of the writing is shown by the fact that the essentials of the first movement at least can be exhibited in melodic outline, without harmony. Its two themes are thus shown in Figure 56.

The buoyant spirits of the opening F major tune are contagious even without its well-nourished harmony; its D major contrast section has almost the sturdiness of a peasant dance, even without the open fifths of the drone bass. As for the second theme, in A major, propounded by the first viola and continued by first violin, it has not only all the Brahmsian subtlety of rhythms of twos and threes contrasted (the contrast is here successive rather than simultaneous) but a simplicity even in all its unexpected turns that makes it sing itself into the inner places of our memories. Closer scrutiny reveals subtle relationships between the two themes, as well as a brevity that packs their significance within smallest compass. Thus the first is announced in only two phrases of four measures each, eight in all. The "contrast" is achieved within five

Theme I.   Figure 56.

a. Allegro non troppo, ma con brio

b. Theme II

more. The usual return requires another eight, into which are
smuggled both a reminiscence of the contrast and an anticipation of the bridge passage that follows Figure 56, a.

In the tonal plans of both themes there are subtleties worth

xamining. Both are determined by the choice Brahms has
ade for the chief tonal contrast of this movement—F major
nd A major, instead of the more usual contrast of F with its
ominant, C. The first theme embodies F, the second A.
ut Brahms wishes to give some subordinate corroborations to
iis fundamental color-contrast; and it is for this reason that
e substitutes for the contrast on the dominant to which he
sually resorts the contrast in D major that here so agree-
oly touches F major with the brighter, fuller tonality. Then,
hen he gets to his second theme, where brilliant A major is
ie prevailing color, he reverses the process, and by skipping
moment to the subdominant D (marked *piano diminuendo*)
id even suggesting the subdominant (G) of this subdominant,
ith a B flat thrown in to darken it still more, and finally
oising *pianissimo* on the chords of D and of B flat, he man-
ges to obscure his brighter key enough to make it warm the
ery cockles of our hearts when it belatedly steals back in
ie cadence.

The most striking feature of the development is the in-
enious and elaborate preparation for the return of the main
ieme, the longest we have yet encountered, that begins at the
iiddle of page 9 in the score. The original motive, rather
esitant in the second violin, *piano*, is carried through five
otes only, and pausing there is fulfilled to a three-measure
hrase by the gay little dance rhythm from the bridge. Again
ie chief motive, more mysterious in its ambiguous diminished-
eventh harmonization; and again the dancing motive. Start-
ng still a third time, the main motive makes its way to a still
ore magically mysterious chord—the dominant seventh of
flat. Note that all the time so far we have been having a
edal point on C, the dominant of the original key, which natu-
lly intensifies our feeling that something is "in the wind,"
aat the theme, in fact, is due to return. As the dancing figure

now expands, the pedal point is abandoned for a moment—but only for a moment. It soon returns, more insistent than ever, and as violin and viola answer second violin and cello in a rapid fire of the first few notes of the motive, in the full sonority of open C's and double-stops that are as satisfying to every true German as beer and sauerkraut, the long-awaited cadence to F major materializes in its full glory, and the fine hearty theme starts off again, made warmer than ever by good ear-filling triplets.

Figure 57

The *Grave ed appassionato* is a tragic poem rising to heights of sustained eloquence, its sombre atmosphere lightened only briefly by the delicate *Allegretto vivace* sections. Its theme is said by Tovey to be taken from a piano saraband written when Brahms was twenty-two. It is certainly deeply Brahmsian in the despairing falls and struggling rises of its melody, in its mingling of the clear strength of major with the melancholy of the minor and of the subdominant in its second phrase, and in its admixture of twos and threes in the division the beats. Figure 57 shows its beginning, transcribed for piano, and its cadence, striking in itself and important for what is to be made from it at the end. It is one of those almost magical distillations of the full quality of a few simple triads, boldly juxtaposed, to which Brahms constantly returns at moments when less shrewd composers would try by the use of chromatics to gild the sun. It extracts the last drop of fatalistic abandon from the succession: C sharp minor tonic, Neapolitan sixth, dominant, tonic—placed low to get the richness of the G- and C-strings and of the close position, and ends with an empty C sharp hollow with hopelessness.

The movement consists of three appearances of this *Grave*, each more impassioned than the last, alternated with the *Allegretto vivace* in lightest A major, and a *Presto* which is only a variation of it. It is the last appearance of the *Grave*, beginning in A major but soon moving back to its native C sharp minor, that brings this grief-burdened music to its full confession, and at the last moment lifts it from deepest clouds into a pale sunshine. Every measure here deserves closest study, but only two of the greatest moments can be illustrated. The first (Figure 58, a) occurs when a sighing figure early transferred in similar fashion from cello to violin is made to rise in increasing intensity from cello to viola, and then to cry out in an agony of dissonances straining away from each other in the two violins. Not all of this wonderful passage, which has Brahms's long breath in fullest measure, can be shown here; but it is cut off at a point that allows one to go directly into the second passage, shown at Figure 58, b. This shows the last dozen measures of the movement, with what is now made of the cadence of simplest triads quoted earlier. Approached from the climbing cantilena of the violins to highest intensity that intermediates between a and b, these chords now seem fuller, darker, more stoically tragic than ever. Sinking lower and lower, first *piano*, then *pianissimo*, they finally fall to a still

Figure 58.

slower alternation, almost all momentum lost, between softest C sharp, now what Tovey calls "a resigned major chord," and A major as "a dark sub-mediant," "the more despairing," as he remarks, "from its having been the tonic chord of the major episodes."

And then, by a stroke as simple as it is unexpected and

profoundly original, the A of the first violin finds itself part of a D minor chord, and climbs up through a slow arpeggio to high A. What is going to happen? Are we to sink back at last to that dark pit of C sharp minor we seem to have escaped? No, A major proves to be the solution of the problem, the issue of the dilemma; and with that pale sunshine which now breaks through the thickest of the clouds, the movement ends with an effect of which Tovey justly says: "Nothing else like this is to be found in music; and it shows what Brahms could achieve by his abstention from all such chromatic resources as could distract attention from the function of simple tonality in sonata form." Atonalists and polytonalists will do well to ponder this passage. It is hard to see how in their monotonous fog they can find anything to solace them for the loss of such rainbows as the one which here, magically emerging from the darkest gloom in which it was all the time implicit, touches it to radiant transfiguration.

Since his experiment in the E minor Cello Sonata, Brahms has not tried again, despite his growing contrapuntal skill, a fugal finale. Here he not only returns to this most difficult of structural types, but achieves an example of it worthy of comparison with such supreme models as Mozart's in the Jupiter Symphony, or Beethoven's in the C major Quartet, Opus 59, No. 3. Indeed, in thematic unity he now excels them both, making nearly every scrap and fragment of the entire piece out of the four measures of fugue theme presented at the start. The idea is to make a whole finale, in the form of a sonata *allegro*, out of a short fugue theme; and a good way to appraise the difficulty of the problem—and the genius of the solution—is to set down the chief variants on a separate sheet (Figure 59), and with this at hand, admire in the score the varied building erected with bricks so curiously alike.

The theme itself (Figure 59, a), expounded as a brief fugue

Figure 59.

on page 29 of the score, owes to its rhythm in equal notes like those of a *perpetuum mobile* an unflagging vigor, and to its motivation a kind of rolling good humor, as of a sailor on a

holiday, which is the prevailing expression of the whole movement. On the second page this good humor is intensified,
chiefly by rhythmic manipulation, until it bursts out, in the
passage marked *ben marcato*, into the emphatic assertiveness
of 59, b. This is an augmentation into three measures of the
first measure only of the theme, and is a good example of the
extraordinary plasticity of a theme in Brahms's hands. By a
turn of the wrist he can make it banteringly jocose or arrogantly
assertive.

All this time the little anacrusis of three rising notes,
C, D, E, that prepare the theme in the very first measure, have
been coming to the fore, until in this acme of the theme's energy they hurl themselves, at the end of each measure, on the
accented note of the next one. Presently, in a moment of relenting energy, these three notes, now made slower and hesitant,
first in cello, then in viola, lay a restraining hand on the racing
music. Each time their original rhythm, as by an irresistible
momentum, reappears in the upper instruments; yet they do
gradually quiet down the pace for the entrance of the second
theme. Now this second theme, sung by the violin (Figure
59, c) turns out to be simply a more tranquil countersubject,
moving mostly in triplets, for the original fugue theme, which
bubbles along below it irrepressibly in the first viola. In other
words, we have here no new theme, but another variant of the
old one, given a new lyric expressiveness by the melodic outline of its counter-theme, by its rhythm (especially the pauses
on the second beats) and by the new, more silvery key of A major. (Note, by the way, that the key-contrast of this finale,
F and A, reflects and corroborates that of the opening *Allegro*.)
In the course of this second theme appears another example of
the sensitiveness to tonal color and contrast so conspicuous
throughout the quintet. Its second half or contrast is pivoted,
as is usual with Brahms, on the dominant, in this case E. This

E opens the door, through the mediant relationship, to two possible keys, C major and C sharp minor, strongly opposed to each other, of course, in coloring. Well, for his evasions just before his cadences, Brahms employs both of these in turn, first C major, then C sharp minor, thus presenting his theme under contrasting illuminations; and not the least wonderful thing about these digressions is their extreme conciseness, the whole of this section of the theme being squeezed into eleven measures. Thematically, it will be noted that this part is a slight elaboration of the slow form of the rising three notes of anacrusis, first appearing during the bridge.

With this the development also begins (top of page 33); but it quickly goes on to something far more striking, to what is indeed the most beautiful and memorable moment of all. This, shown with its harmony at Figure 59, d, may be enjoyed naïvely for its tender expression, its sensitive utterance, before we look at it more analytically, and see that *it is nothing but the outline of the fugue theme, softened by minor mode, by chromatic harmony, by triplet rhythm!* Surely this is the most incredible of all the variants of this Protean theme. Who would have imagined that that Sancho Panza of a tune, verging on the vulgar in its robust good humor, could possibly be sensitized to such quixotic chivalry, elegance, and grace? Strauss has embodied in two themes of his "Don Quixote" these extreme types of human nature; Brahms makes one root-theme suffice for both.

In the coda, *Presto,* 9–8, the little three-note anacrusis, of which we have already noted the gradually waxing importance, occupies by itself two whole measures of the six now required to hold the theme (Figure 59, e, shows the second phrase, which is in F, rather than the first in B flat, in order to facilitate comparison with the other excerpts). Following this, after viola and cello have played pitch-and-toss with the rest of the theme, they join in a still more vigorous scramble upwards, from their lowest C's, on the same expanded anacrusis, to some widespread, sustained chords that warn us to "look out for trouble." By this time it has all become so wild and care-free, and we so excited, that when the "acme" of the theme (the augmentation of its first measure into three) reappears in more triumphant mood than ever, and almost falls over itself in the three beats to a measure which are all it has now to disport itself in, we are not in the least worried, but if anything only more elated than before; and we feel, as the whole ends with a mad rush back to F, and a crash and a bang, that, as the newspapers say, "a good time was had by all."

CHAPTER XVI

THE CELLO SONATA IN F MAJOR, OPUS 99

In writing his second sonata for the cello—a more difficult instrument to combine satisfactorily with the piano than the violin, or, for that matter, the clarinet—Brahms shows himself more skillful in making each part effective in itself, and especially in its relation to the other, than in the earlier sonata. First of all, the cello part is written on the whole in a higher register; where the lower register is used, as in the mysterious approach to the return of the main theme in the *Allegro*, or in the beautiful plucked basses of the *Adagio*, it is with a keener instinct for its exact dramatic effect; and while there is here perhaps no single theme lovelier than the song for the lowest strings with which the first sonata opens, muddy places such as mar that sonata are never found, and the general sonority is transparent, brilliant where brilliance is needed, and everywhere clear.

The habit of conceiving the two instruments as coöperating equals is in evidence almost from the start. In the first few measures, to be sure, the piano gives only background, in tremolo chords, for the salient outlining in high register by the cello of those bold leaps to F, to G, and to C, which at once proclaim that this music is to be stormy and passionate. But these measures, characteristically impassioned as they are in expression, are from the standpoint of form preliminary, or at least incomplete. The real business begins to be transacted only when, in the ninth measure, in the immensely vigorous passage skeletonized to its essentials in Figure 60, a, the piano opposes to these bold leapings of the cello a countersubject of its own that in its steady downward march of six quarter-notes is scarcely less bold. The true theme of the sonata is thus neither a melody with accompaniment, as in the first sonata, nor even either one of these two energetic themes by itself; it is the two in their opposition and mutual completion—a bit of rugged two-part counterpoint in which the explosive energy of the oddly rhythmed leaps is controlled by the dogged energy of the even quarters. These implacable quarters, it will be noted,—these quarters that seem to belie their name by crying "No quarter!" at every step,—begin on the tonic F and reach the dominant C, thus equilibrating firmly the whole theme in the central key, F major.

The passionately troubled character of the main theme is clarified only for a moment in the more frank, not to say head-long second theme in C major which the piano presently con-tributes. The cello takes it up in all its candid clarity, but soon carries it into minor keys and more fragmentary rhythms, and before long reverts to the struggling expression of the main theme in a cantilena in A minor which even brings back the very quarter-notes of the former motive. It may be observed that they now start on the third step of A minor (instead of on the tonic of F as before) and later, when the piano takes them up, on its fifth step, and are therefore more insistent and relentless than ever. This for the moment however ex-hausts their passion, and they fade toward silence in the in-genious two-string passage for the cello which closes this section.

With the change of signature to three sharps and the start of the development their energy revives. The two halves of the theme are now combined in a new way, successively instead of simultaneously, in the passage shown at 60, b. This results

Figure 60.

in eliminating the leaping motive in favor of the quarter-note motive, which however changes its character, through diminution from quarters to eighths, and for a page or more substitutes a wandering restlessness for its former assurance. With the two measures of tremolo for cello, dying from *fortissimo* to *pianissimo*, the mood changes to one of foreboding hush, and the first motive resumes its priority. Its character is for the moment entirely changed; its impatient leaps are quieted to the questioning tentativeness of quarter-notes and halves in the piano, and finally to dotted half-notes, one to each measure, that while almost losing all rhythmic momentum nevertheless outline the theme in dim silhouette (Figure 60, c). Traffic has now almost ceased; yet in this pause we feel sure that all the passionate energy is to be renewed, even if we do not quite see how. Then the left hand of the piano timidly suggests three notes of the quarter-note motive, placed on a suspensive harmony that points to F major, but does not yet assert it (Figure 60, d). The right hand agrees, the cello also. More and more confident, the piano plays the whole motive downward from high D, broadening out at last to a cadence that ushers in both the tonic of F major and the theme in all its pristine vigor. . . . The last excerpt in Figure 60—excerpt e—shows the ultimate quietude reached by both themes in the coda. The leaps have been toned down to rhythmic tranquillity and tonal repose in the piano. The scale suggested by the quarter-notes has become complete, begun by the cello, finished by the piano down to the low F. This virtually completes the substance of the music; but the prevailing emotional tone of the movement is restored (in amusingly literal agreement with the formula for the Brahmsian coda we worked out in our first chapter) by a brief "sprint" at the very end.

The *Adagio affetuoso* is a lovely poem, as lyrical and as richly contemplative as we may expect from the composer of the great songs from "Liebestreu" to "Immer leiser wird mein Schlummer." What gives it an incomparable eloquence is the freedom of its declamation, the arrangement of the melodic motives never in a stiff predetermined pattern, but according to the ebb and flow of feeling, here broadening out in noble dignity, there condensing to a rapid insistence. This freedom of declamation is of course dependent on the contrapuntal skill now attained—no composer whose counterpoint is not skillful can possibly achieve this sort of flexibility.

Take as an instance the very opening phrase of the main theme, freely transcribed for piano alone in Figure 61, a. Only for the first few notes does the melody proceed straight away; by the end of the second measure the texture begins to be made of extraordinarily free and expressive imitations of the little figure of three sixteenth notes leading into an eighth, indicated by brackets, and derived from the notes of the plucked cello at the very beginning. In the second phrase, starting in the fifth measure and extended, according to Brahms's later manner, to no less than seven measures, the melody goes over to the cello, while the figure originally plucked is taken up by the piano; but from the second measure of this phrase also the texture becomes freely imitative, and, as the brackets bear witness, marvellously flexible. The crescendo to the *forte* is given increasing momentum by the condensation of four sixteenths to two; once the C sharp is reached it is broadened out to a whole measure, over changing harmonies that multiply its expressiveness; in the fifth measure the sixteenth-notes expand from four to six; and, most beautiful of all, the cadence is given ineffable earnestness by the augmentation of these six into notes twice as long. (Does not this kind of augmentation give a little the intensity that biblical verse gets by repetition?—"For lo, thine enemies, O Lord, lo, thine enemies shall perish; and all the workers of wickedness shall be destroyed.") This first part of the movement is completed by the lovely bit of fluent innocence, as of a candid child, shown in Figure 61, b.

Part II, in the sombre key of F minor, is chiefly devoted to

Figure 61

the development of still a third theme, on a motive (Figure 61, c) as earnest as the first, but unlike that tinged with deep melancholy. In all this part, and in the ingenious preparation for return to the main theme where its motive of sixteenth-notes is plucked by the cello in different registers, with subtly changing harmonies from the piano, we cannot but wonder at the resourcefulness with which the composer turns such brief motives to such varied, ever interesting uses.

Figure 62

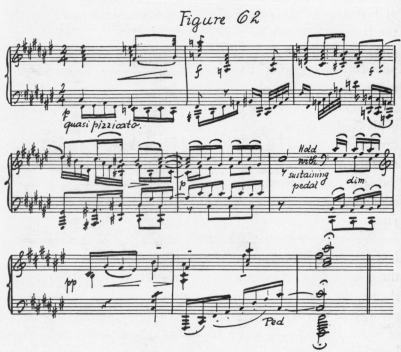

The supreme marvel comes at the end, where in nine measures of coda he manages not only to touch on all the main ideas, but by one means or another to enhance the significance of each. The sustained motive in the piano begins this time (Figure 62) not from the fifth, C sharp, but from the tonic itself, F sharp. This gives it a new decisiveness and finality. The cello *pizzicati*, too, become more agitated in rhythm and more dramatic in harmony; and as they swarm the ramparts, first to F sharp and then to high D, the piano adds the other, melancholy motive the cello had in Figure 61, c. The cello answers in even more impassioned accents, but instead of ending the movement on this strenuous note relents, and falls away to *piano* and to the earlier childlike, innocent theme. On the dying pulsations of this, gravitated now to the central key of F sharp, the movement sinks toward its conclusion. Just at the last moment, the cello adds the characteristic curve of the melancholy motive, its melancholy changed to a stoical calm, a peaceful tranquillity. The quiet arpeggio of F sharp major brings the final chord.

The shrewdness with which the scherzo, *Allegro passionato*, is planned to make the most of the somewhat limited technical capacities of the violoncello as an instrument, while dealing tactfully with its many disabilities and shortcomings, will amuse the observant student. The very melodic outline of the theme is planned for it, consisting as it does of pivotal notes with adjacent steps such as the cellist can easily manage with two fingers—though it is mostly in the second half of this lavishly laid out scherzo, say from the one sharp signature on, that these advantages are reaped. At the start the piano has the theme, the cello does subordinate work, though even here the pivoting of its part around C gives it a certain continuity, a sort of sonorous centre. When it takes up the theme for itself, the lengthening out of certain notes which we saw Brahms adopting as early as the Horn Trio for purposes of development, gives it halting places that are most welcome, both to technic and to tone. At the second soft entrance of the theme the cello has first pedal-point, and then the arrested notes again, both of which it finds effective; while as soon as it is entrusted with the whole of the theme it can whisper it out in mysterious *piano* or saw it away in carefree *fortissimo* with equal ease. As for the trio, at once one of the broadest and the most concise of Brahms's tunes, mostly on the A string, it is a cellist's holiday. Thus throughout this movement there are few of those places, unhappily frequent in most music for the cello, that sound so difficult that you wish, with Dr. Johnson, they were impossible.

The finale is a short, spirited, and highly effective rondo on a theme of folk-like character. Despite the fact that the second theme is one of those rather manufactured bits that Brahms occasionally allows to pass his censorship, and that the conclusion theme has little more individuality, the main theme is fortunately so attractive in itself, and so attractively and variously set for the instruments, that it suffices for the entertainment. Towards the middle of the movement, at the five flat signature, occurs an episode more serious than the rest, in B flat minor, the theme of which may seem at first of dubious origin. Whence comes it? Examination will show that, in order to produce it, the main theme has been changed from major to minor, and has had its rhythm reduced from quadruple to triple division of the beat. This process curiously parallels the treatment at a similar place in the finale of the F major Quintet, and affords a new instance of the plasticity of all themes to Brahms's later technique.

CHAPTER XVII

THE VIOLIN SONATA IN A MAJOR, OPUS 100

THE proper retort to those who over-insist on the chance resemblance between the chief theme of the A major Sonata and Wagner's "Prize Song" is Brahms's own "Any fool can see that." We shall here refer to that theme as "The Prize Song Theme," in the hope of shaming those who see in the use of four such notes by a composer any more "plagiarism" than there is in the use by a writer of any commonly associated four words. Within the twenty measures shown in Figure 63 the motive becomes so completely Brahmsian that the Prize Song is quite forgotten by all who listen for music rather than in order to display their own cleverness in discovering insignificant tags.

That this is achieved mostly through rhythmic means we shall be able to convince ourselves by a simple analysis, well worth making as a vivid object lesson in what stamps quite common material with individuality. The piano alone announces the first four-measure phrase, to which the violin responds with a one-measure echo of its cadence that would have occurred to few composers but Brahms. Another four are echoed in the same way in one. In the eleventh measure the piano begins to play with the motive, shortening it to three notes, which by measure 13 have boiled down to two, followed by four. Three of these are echoed by violin as in previous phrases. The last five measures of the illustration (and of the theme) are devoted to a more sustained melodic cadence, with,

in the last three, an extension that adds one final delightful
touch of flexibility to the rhythmic plan.

Now note: this tune essentially consists, like thousands of
folk-songs, of four phrases of four measures each, balanced
in pairs, the first two presenting the musical idea, the third

Allegro amabile.   Figure 63.

offering a contrast, and the last cadencing. But the echoes and
extensions Brahms has added in its course give it a delightful
variety, measures 5, 10, and 15 providing single-measure echoes
that break up the square-cut monotony of the four-measure
phrases, and measure 19 stretching the last of these to five
measures. Suppose we plot the finished theme, as follows:

Phrase 1: Measures 1–4. Echo, Meas. 5.
Phrase 2: Measures 6–9. Echo, Meas. 10.
Phrase 3: Measures 11–14. Echo, Meas. 15.
Phrase 4: Measures 16, 17, 18, 20. Extended by 19.

We find that all we have to do in order to gain a vivid sense of the difference between this beautifully flexible treatment and the literalness of the *routinier* and the bungler is to omit the "irregularities" (that is, the genius!) of the measures in the right hand column, and play only the measures in the centre column. So doing, we shall have the salutary experience of reducing Brahms's distinction, so far as we may, to vulgarity— though even then there will remain in Phrase 3 some interstitial genius that will defeat our most honest efforts.

The bass of a theme is often quite as important as its melody, sometimes more so, as conveying to us more unequivocally its harmonic foundation. In the present theme the four opening notes of the bass, progressing so sturdily stepwise up the diatonic scale, one note to each beat, are as essential as the Prize-song intervals of the treble; to its "amiability" (the tempo indication *Allegro amabile* is here peculiarly happy) they add a quiet, self-confident strength. We shall meet them again.

The second theme, shown at Figure 64, a, and the third or conclusion theme (64, b) present several new rhythms, devised to contrast with and complement the straightforward thetic Prize-song motive. II, appropriately marked *teneramente,* opens with tenderest, almost caressing anacruses, each of which, after the first, lasts half a measure, and not only resolves a preceding suspension but leads up to a new one—all the suspensions falling on accented beats. From this construction the tune derives great continuity and lyric warmth. Towards the end of the part quoted the feeling becomes more emphatic, and we find a new motive, thetic once more, and the accent strongly marked (a quarter-note twice dotted, followed by the jerk of a sixteenth and a quarter). These three notes, raised to high voltage, so to speak, by the double dot, form a motive of strongest emphasis, upon which much later development depends.

After half a page of dallying with the Prize-song theme in retrospective mood, the composer starts in on the serious busi-

Figure 64.

ness of development with some bold polyphonic combinations of its opening four notes. These are placed in all possible positions, beginning on each of the three beats in succession, turned upside down, and finally "diminished" to eighth-notes, in the piano, against the two quarters and triplet of the conclusion theme which somewhat unexpectedly make their appearance in the violin. Once there they too begin to be roughly tossed about, from part to part and from beat to beat. A pause in this highly athletic badinage comes only when the violin insists on the two quarters, softer and softer, while the piano sinks toward silence.

Now comes a new mood. The piano offers an insinuatingly gracious version of the conclusion theme, in C sharp minor, made into a complete song-like phrase, while the violin supplies quiet background. It is only when the violin itself takes up the same cajoling, almost wheedling form of this melody that we begin to see beyond it to something new; for the countersubject now brought by the piano is made of those same fluent, plausible triplets, and now they are going up along the scale in a fashion that suggests coming change. Sure enough, in a moment the three notes change from three to a beat to two to a beat, and then, in a highly Brahmsian hobbling figure, to three to two beats, or, if we wish to be finically mathematical, one and a half to a beat. Slower and slower, we see; and meanwhile, as they steady down for business, the two quarters of the other motive, in the violin, are getting weaker and weaker, gradually being eliminated from the picture, until nothing is left of them but a sort of audible pause, on low C sharp. And then the theme enters, *dolce*, in the original A major, with as innocent an air of "Well, here I am, just in case you should want me," as if its creator had not all this time been preparing by slowing up the rhythm of those triplets for just this very bass that they have inevitably ushered in! . . .

It is only towards the end of the movement that the emphatic motive with the double dots begins to expand. When it reappears in the violin, near the end of theme II, it is deflected so as to reach, with a feeling of greater tension than before, the subdominant key, D, instead of the tonic. The conclusion theme is strongly if briefly urged by the piano, *forte* and with accents, but after a few measures falls to a sudden hush. What is going to happen? On its lowest string, darkly and mysteriously, the violin propounds two very long notes (lasting two whole measures each) which we recognize as a questioning form of the emphatic motive, now deprived of its vigorous double dots and suppressed to *sotto voce*. Its haunting mystery is deepened by strange, wide-spread, slowly-built harmonies in the piano. The sudden hush of it all is like going from full sunlight into a dim-lit shadowy cave. The violin again sounds the motive, not quite so slowly but still in wide, sustained tones, while gradually the harmony goes down and down toward the subdominant side of the key, from A to D, then to G, finally even to C. Only then, with the *vivace*, the original double-dotted rhythm of the motive reappears and the music slowly climbs out of its dark subdominant cave into the sunlight again, and to its last soaring assertion of the theme in clearest A major. . . .

The structural idea in all the "portmanteau movements" of Brahms is to combine lyric melody in one theme with rhythmic activity in another, unifying the two through some sort of metrical equivalence. Though the present *Andante tranquillo* is notated in 2–4 measure, the interlinking of its harmonies, especially at the cadences, indicates that its true unit of movement is the eighth-note. Only by counting eighths, or at least feeling them, do we get the right sense of its undulating motion, carried along on a sort of gentle ground swell, of its caressing figures in the piano, and of the innocent final cadence of its last three measures, pausing on a question. The section is essentially lyric. To it as it pauses on its innocent question comes, on the very notes it has used to frame it, A and D, the whimsical answer of the *Vivace*, 3–4, its measure equal to the single beat of the *Andante*. What a charming badinage is this *Vivace*, perverse as mischief, light as laughter! For its first appearance it carries a tune, of folk character like the other; but this tune is hardly more than a froth on the surface of its dashing current; and we feel from the first, in those *staccato* jumps of the violin away from the heavy beat, and in the funny dancing in one chord marked *piano leggiero*, that its main business is to make a carnival of rhythm.

The melodic idea returns, in D major now, and more serious and eloquent than before. . . . As in a conversation,

a. Allegretto grazioso. Figure 65.

where the seriousness of one person only exasperates the mad-cap humor of another, the *Vivace* now breaks in at a livelier pace than before, and without even pretending to clothe itself in melody dances off to pursue its rhythmic carnival in pluckings of the violin and little dry pecks (*senza Pedale*) of the piano. It goes through exactly its former steps, but it has now taken off its flesh and is dancing in its bones. Once more returns the *Andante*, reduced for its last appearance to its lowest terms, its questioning cadence A, D, sounding now more hesitantly than ever, on the piano only, on weak beats, while the double-stops of the violin settle toward silence. But the *Vivace*, the more full-blooded of the two elements, must have the final word; and this it takes in one brief but triumphant swoop.

The contrast between the opening and closing pages of the finale is almost as striking as if the composer had planned a poem of youth and age; the hero loses in the course of the drama all his aggressiveness, though he remains as noble at the end as he was at the beginning. This heroic theme (Figure 65, a) is music of full daylight, of active life, of buoyant confidence. The first shadow of doubt is thrown by the diminished seventh chord that ripples up from its final cadence, and the foreboding mood thus suggested haunts the whole of the second theme, and is intensified when, after the first return of the main theme, the violin introduces the hesitant motive of eighths shown at Figure 65, b, first on a suspensive harmony, later with a sense of heavy weariness on the tonic of F sharp minor (65, c). From this moment the uncertainty of those dipping eighth-notes more and more undermines the confidence of the initial theme. In the coda the two motives at last appear together, as at 65, d, a subtle combination of the dubiety of the dipping eighths with the chastened but still virile confidence of the main theme. As so often in the Brahmsian codas, it is only in this last incarnation that the theme reveals its full individuality, as an old man, even in his failing strength, seems sometimes more fully himself than he ever could be in the thoughtless overflowing energy of youth.

CHAPTER XVIII

THE TRIO IN C MINOR, OPUS 101

In none of his works in C minor, embodying his famous "C minor mood" of dark and passionate struggle,—not in the first string quartet, not in the third piano quartet, not even in the First Symphony,—has Brahms created in terms of this sombre tonality a more characteristically dramatic piece than the Opus 101 Trio. It is a mature version, stronger, surer, starker, of the same drama the Piano Quartet suggests in accents of youthful trouble and uncertainty. The opening *Allegros* of the two works are as strikingly alike in atmosphere as they are strikingly unlike in emotional and intellectual concentration. Both open in the mood of stormy passion, that of the Quartet more grievously and heavily, that of the Trio with an almost desperate energy. Both end in dejection, weary yet grimly stoic.

But that of the Trio is far more mature in its relentless directness and conciseness. It has no room for digressions; its intensity never abates; its varied stages of emotion are all unified not only by its sombre tonal atmosphere but by actual motivation: its motives, in fact, thanks to the flexibility their creator has now attained, grow out of each other. Practically the whole movement is already present *in posse* in the rising triplet of the first measure in the bass. Figures 66 and 67 set down the chief adventures of this generating triplet, 66 showing the themes themselves, 67 their developments. The mainspring that starts the whole action is coiled in the aggressive triplets of the opening measures (66, a), carrying first the bass up from C to E flat, and then the treble from E flat to the apex G. About a page is devoted to this motive and to a vigor-

Figure 66.

ous antithetic one in broken, detached rhythms; and when a cadence in C minor has been reached, and it is time to move toward the contrasting key of E flat, the bridge is made from nothing new, but with powerful economy from the same heaven-assailing triplets (66, b). Even the second theme itself

(66, c) also proceeds from them, but by a rhythmic augmentation to quarter-notes that transforms their galvanic energy to a lower voltage—to a kind of quiet determination, or noble staunchness. There is a severity in the writing here that matches this nobility: the two strings have the even-paced melody in octaves that give an effect almost as plain as unisons; against them the piano, also in plain unisons, gives the fewest possible notes to complete the harmonies.

A version of the first theme, with its triplets augmented to quarter-notes (Figure 67, a) suggestive also of the second,

Figure 67.

opens the development section with great power. Presently this abates to the initial rhythmic form, but now with an expression altered from fierce resolution to graceful dallying (67, b). This in turn, by a highly Brahmsian transfer of the triplet to the first beat (67, c), becomes positively genial, even sunny, in a way we should not have believed possible, especially in its continuation in major mode by the piano. But all this, however charming, is no more than a pale glint of sun on a stormy winter afternoon. With the irruption of the motive in broken rhythms returns the turmoil in which the development culminates.

It is only in the coda that this struggle finally exhausts itself, and a new augmentation, paralyzing the energy of the initial triplet, makes the theme too heavy to rise from the E flat to the apex G, and forces it instead to gravitate to the tonic C (Figure 67, d). Still longer augmentations, into quarter- and half-notes, keep it poising upon the E flat as if in a vain effort to surmount it, and bring it at last to the final C with an indescribable effect of having been engulfed by weariness. Thus there is in this movement an incomparable tragic unity; one motive permeates it from beginning to end, as one action permeates a Greek tragedy; the sad final descent to the key-note, the two brusque chords that cut it off, are only the completion of the long arch of the curve that rose so buoyantly in the opening triplets. The grief so poignant in the emotion is matched by the strength of the thought.

Grievous emotion and strong thought—to what extent is this combination increasingly characteristic of Brahms as the tale of his works extends, and as he approaches his last years? And how far do these general traits tend to express themselves in certain recurring inflections in his actual thematic texture? It is certainly striking that this stormy *Allegro energico* should end, its energy all dissipated, with the same heavy rise from the tonic and weary redescent to it that we noted in the variation theme of the C major Trio, written when its composer had just turned fifty. We cannot fail to be struck even more forcibly, therefore, when in the delightful *Presto non assai* that now follows we find in the elusive muted strings the same rise to minor third and descent to tonic, with in the piano part further descent through various resting points to the low tonic. Is not melancholy the very breath of these intervals, even though it be here lightened from tragic grief to tender wistfulness?

From these literal resemblances, however, the importance of which it is so easy to overrate, we may turn to the more vital question of what Brahms does with his tender theme, of how he makes it gradually disengage so fairy-like a charm. First of all, there is an irresistible delight in the form of the whole movement, not to be felt in any short quotation, but due to the neat precision with which it divides into two roughly equal halves, marked by three identical cadences, one on C, and one on G, and a third on C again. Even in so short a bit as Figure 68, showing the first half, rounded by the cadences on C and on G, the joy of this delicate balance can be felt.

A second charm is the subtlety of the relation between the four note refrain of the strings, thrice repeated, given to the right hand in our piano transcription, and the flowing piano part represented by the left hand. We saw in Chapter IV how a single note could be given inexhaustible musical interest by repetition in changing contexts. Here the repeated element is a whole refrain rather than a single note, and the fact that it falls into unisons with the other part in the first measure, into sixths in the second, into thirds in the third, and even more that its harmonic implications change, give it endless fascination. Somewhat similar is the charm that is felt in the elusive difference between two forms of nearly the same melodic phrase, first as harmonized in measures 4–8, then as in 8–12. But it is vain to particularize the beauties of the treatment here; our sense of its elusiveness and yet of its logical necessity and exact rightness, seems to be enhanced at every measure; and our efforts at analysis are apt in the end to fall back on the blanket phrase offered so long ago by Gurney

Figure 68.

in his *The Power of Sound*—that the beauty lies in "the way the notes go."

The trio presents fascinating Brahmsian subtleties of rhythm. Each three-measure phrase of it (See Figure 69) commences tentatively on a half-note anacrusis, tied over so as to take the accent away from the normal place and give an effect of syncopation. A second chord, also syncopated, is given great emphasis by plucked eighths crossing over from cello to violin, and culminating in the three staccato chords that bring the curiously neat cadence. The first, second, and last of these cadences centre respectively on the fifth, third, and the first step of F minor, thus echoing and corroborating the "tragic motive" already heard in the scherzo refrain.

After the repetition of the scherzo, a one-page coda returns even more strongly to this tragic motive. It is felt behind all the imitations of strings and piano with which this begins; it is felt even more unequivocally in those solemn augmentations of the last thirteen measures, where the two strings make for the last time their struggling ascent to the third and their

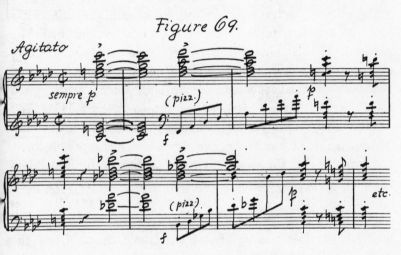

Figure 69.

weary fall back to the tonic, and at last to the low dominant. This passage sounds for all the world like one of the Serious Songs—and it is in a scherzo!

In the *Andante grazioso* melancholy gives place to a cheerful folk-song mood. The rhythm is again striking. This time Brahms is making one of his few experiments in combining duple and triple measure, building one measure of three quarter-notes and two of two quarters each into a motive that is as natural and suave as it is quaint and memorable. It will be noticed that the changes of harmony determine these uneven groupings of beats so unequivocally that even were there no bar-lines we could hardly hear them differently.

The charmingly naïve phrases thus produced are linked together with an equal simplicity. The scheme is a three-part tune. Violin and cello present the first part, immediately repeated by the piano. The two strings play the second and third parts (the third of course a return to the first), and the piano echoes these as well. Omitting the piano repetitions, easily supplied from the miniature score, we may set down the string sections in transcription for piano in Figure 70. How gracious are the falling two-beat groups in the first two phrases! How innocent almost to childishness is the sequence up one step in the third measure of Part II, and the poising on Brahms's beloved subdominant seventh chord with raised fourth step linking it close to the return in Part III! And in that, how simple yet expressive is the sequence to the subdominant that at last brings two three-beat measures together, and how playful the slight rhythmic ambiguity Brahms teases us with in the last four measures, where his favorite subdominant sevenths recur! Are they—so he quizzically asks us—are they four measures of 2–4 with a feminine cadence in the last, or does the weight of that tonic chord throw the three preceding beats into one more 3–4 measure, echoing the two we heard a moment back? It is the kind of delicate equivocation that we are as content to leave unsolved as to solve— and he leaves us guessing.

The finale is a brilliant, highly effective movement, *Allegro molto*, on a theme of great rhythmic energy, which reaches its acme, in its seventh and eighth measures, in a motive of four strongly accented notes. We are made aware, from the very beginning of the brief contrast that immediately follows, pivoted on the dominant according to Brahms's habit, that this motive is to be of peculiar importance. Within the quiet second theme we discern it in hiding; it seems in some elusive way to have entered into the substance of the rolling figures for the piano marked *meno Allegro;* and as this section grad-

Figure 70.

Part I. *(played by strings.) repeated by Piano.*

Andante grazioso.

Parts II and III, *also played by strings, repeated by Piano.*

ually dies away it sallies forth unmistakably from the strings. In the development we find it subjected to that curious process of lengthening out a single note in a theme that Brahms has used from time to time ever since the earliest example we noted in the Horn Trio: this augments it, at the bottom of page 30, to four measures. Finally, in the coda, which changes the main theme from minor to major and churns it into great agitation, this same four-measure augmentation provides a long and exciting climax up to the hurdle-race between all three instruments with which the work closes.

IV

THE LAST YEARS

FACSIMILE OF THE OPENING OF THE CLARINET QUINTET

(Courtesy of the *Gesellschaft der Musikfreunde*, Vienna.)

The rapid method of making half-notes, pointed out in the facsimile from the C minor Quartet, may be even better observed here in the high A of the clarinet in the sixth measure. At the end of the same measure, observe how the tie is carried only a short distance to the left from the second note. It is not needed as long as the first note sounds; and if it extended further to the left it would clutter the page to no purpose. The same dealing with ties may be observed in Wagner's highly neat and practical manuscripts.

Far more significant than any such details of writing is the change that this sketch shows to have been made in the first important cadence. Measures 10–11, stricken across with pencil lines, are replaced by four measures that vastly improve upon them in at least three respects. 1). The adopted version gives the cadence greater rhythmic expansion, deliberation: the clarinet, coming upon the stage, holds our attention more satisfyingly before it is replaced by other matters. 2). Instrumentally the new version is better because, taking the clarinet to its high B, it allows it to spread out virtually its entire gamut, to its lowest note, in beautifully shaded tone-color. 3). Above all it is better in harmony, that is to say, in this case, in composition, because for a rather tame tonic second inversion ("six-four chord") it substitutes four measures of vigorous and various subdominant chords, which make an impressive portico to the reappearance of one of the main motives.

The substituted measures are the tenth to the thirteenth in Figure 87, where their effect can be conveniently tried out.

CHAPTER XIX

THE VIOLIN SONATA IN D MINOR, OPUS 108

In Brahms's latest period the continually growing intellectual and emotional concentration of his music reaches its acme in such masterpieces as the last violin sonata, the second viola quintet, and (despite its slightly less fresh thematic substance) the Clarinet Quintet. In these works supreme mastery attains its moment of equilibrium with temperamental vitality, before that is touched by the inevitable waning of energy of old age.

Thus all of the most essential material of the opening *Allegro* of the D minor Sonata (with the exception of the purely subordinate and lyrical second and conclusion themes) is contained within the first four measures of the main theme, transcribed for piano in Figure 71, a. First there is the motive that rises a fourth from A to D, and turning in a characteristic group of eighth-notes falls back to A. It has some of the weariness characteristic of motives that rise from and fall back to a single central note. It is immediately followed by the curious oscillation from the A, a double-dotted half-note, to the very short G, and back again, which is to play an important part in the development. As we are dealing with so strongly contrapuntal a mind, we shall expect the bass to prove little less important than the treble; and noting the characteristic figure that descends from A to low C in the first two measures, beginning with an even-paced scale, we shall soon find that this is a third motive of major interest.

Figure 71.

The first estate of the main theme, we note, is quiet, smooth, evenly gliding; the characteristic hobbling rhythm of the accompaniment suggests a furtive, almost stealthy movement, which the marking *piano, sotto voce* corroborates; and although the long A's of the third and fourth measures already oscillate towards different keys—one towards F, the other towards D minor—they move less boldly than they will later. In short, the whole air of this first statement is suppressed, mysterious, provocative. It piques our curiosity, makes us feel that a drama of wide issues is commencing.

If we compare this preliminary statement with the form the theme takes on as early as the twenty-first measure, in its first important cadence (Figure 71, b) we shall already get a strong sense of its latent possibilities. Here the originally mild, suave, resolution of its third measure on the A as mediant of F is already replaced by a much bolder progression: the A now reached is the more vigorous tonic of A major, while the D from which it cadences is harmonized with the seventh-chord on B, far more active than the early triad of D minor. At the same time the bass leaves its groping along the scale for a much more assertive descent by thirds which conducts the harmony resolutely to the cadence. In other words, the theme is already beginning to act. And in the bridge passage which immediately follows (71, c) this action becomes even more energetic. The A expands itself to two measures, with urgent reiteration. The eighth-note figure goes into the accompaniment and, combined with syncopations, propels the whole powerfully forward. The descending thirds of the bass change from half-notes to more insistent quarters, and extend their line further, moving, now in the alto voice, from high D down to C sharp. The theme has put off all its pristine reserve, and become strenuously active.

In the development section, however, one of the most extraordinary ever conceived, remaining as it does for its whole duration of forty-six measures entirely on a pedal point A, the theme resumes, and even deepens, its veiled and cryptic reticence. While the piano, in a scarcely audible *pianissimo*, initiates the hypnotic A's, four even quarters to a bar, that are to pulsate relentlessly through two pages, the violin plays, *molto piano e sotto voce sempre,* a form of the theme ingeniously adapted to two strings, in such fashion that the upper plays the original rising-fourth motive, and the lower the original bass motive, (71, d) while both necessarily sound on a monotonous level of tone, without nuance. This absence of accent, a sort of studious understatement that makes the harmonic temerities strike us all the more because none of them are emphasized and we have to determine their relative importance for ourselves, persists throughout the development.

There is such kaleidoscopic, ever-changing beauty in this development, and it all comes so inevitably yet with such welling imagination from the three motives, that it is impossible here to do more than suggest its richness. Each hearer must taste the specific beauties for himself. Nevertheless he may find assistance in a tabular view that points to some of the more striking features. Numbering the forty-six measures of the development section (beginning at the light double-bar), and indicating major keys with capital letters, minor keys with small letters, chords with Roman numerals (I for tonic, V for dominant, etc.) and scale-steps with Arabic numerals (as 3 for mediant, 7 for leading-tone, etc.) we get the following

TABULAR VIEW OF DEVELOPMENT SECTION

Measures

1– 2	d V. Motives 1 and 3 (bass motive) in violin, on two strings.
3– 4	Imitation by piano.
5– 8	Imitations from instrument to instrument of eighth-note figure from Motive 1.
9–12	Motive 2 (Oscillation from double-dotted half note) d V, A I, and a I.

13–24   Repetition of 1–12, now beginning on a V. In measure 21, the double-dotted notes go into the tenor voice, and the harmony goes to g V.

25   The second and third measures of the main motive are tranquillized to the three descending half-notes for the violin, from which exhales a lovely quietude.

29–30   The restlessness returns with the oscillating motive and the strikingly new and sudden harmonic coloring of F sharp minor. Harmony F sharp, I, 3.

31–32   The same, but now A I, 3.
With the sudden *dolce* of measure 33 begins the long descent to the recapitulation.

37–44   Motive 3 goes into the violin, which descends from high E to its lowest notes, first on d V, then on g V (the touch of subdominant giving the feeling of approaching rest.)

45–46   Motive 3, in piano, augmented to half-note values, in dying momentum. d V.

All through these almost dizzying transformations of key and motive, it must be remembered, the four quarter-note A's sound relentlessly from the piano. They are the point of reference by which we measure such extreme changes of coloring as that from F, where the A is major third, to F sharp minor, where the A is minor third. They are the anchor of our captive balloon, which for the rest floats freely in the sunlight or among the clouds, letting us penetrate ever new vistas of landscape, now smiling, now darkling. . . .

The even rippling of eighth-notes which has contributed so much, throughout the development, to the hypnotic effect of the reiterant A's, continues even in the recapitulation up

to the very verge of the cadence to the bridge passage, shown
in its original form at 71, b but now made more passionate by
transference to the G string. But with the bridge itself there
comes a complete and necessary change of mood. Hypnosis,
whatever its charm, cannot last indefinitely without merging
into sleep. So Brahms wakes us up by a sudden return to the
staccato utterance and the vigorously-stepping thirds of 71, c.
They now extend the range of their march, moving, it will
be seen, boldly enough (in 71, e), and with eighth-rests that
multiply their energy. In this way the healthy tone of alert-
ness is restored after the languor of the development, and before the return of the more lyric second and third themes.

Figure 72.

One further transformation of the main motive remains
in reserve—fittingly, the most impressive of all. It comes as
the final word, after the shorter tonic pedal point on D has
balanced and corroborated that of the development on A. This
persistent D, of course, attunes our minds for the end; it is
naturally harmonized largely with the subdominant, always

charged with the sense of conclusion. Thus when we arrive, after deftly-arranged half-measure pauses in the rhythm, at the last seven measures, arranged for piano alone in Figure 72, we await the *Nunc dimittis*. It comes with one of those magical flashes of genius that are as simple as they are sublime. For the first time, the D of the upward-fourth motive is no longer the reposeful D of the tonic of D minor. It is now at last the intensely dynamic D of the dominant of G minor, the subdominant key. And the A to which it falls is no longer the mild third-step of F major, as at first, nor even the rather sad but resigned root of the dominant chord of D minor of the bridge cadence. It is now the fifth of the tonic-chord, but of D major, not D minor. It combines, that is to say, the finality of tonic harmony with the suggestion of questioning, of further possibilities, of the fifth step; and both of these it combines with the generous warmth of D major. Still further to emphasize this new-found contentment and warmth, the second measure of the original motive is repeated in three different registers, ending in the full glow of the G string and with the piano backing it with a rich arpeggio of D major, in all the deliberation of triplet motion. It is the perfect, broad, happy cadence for a nobly-planned movement.

The *Adagio*, fittingly after so complex a movement as the first, takes a form exceedingly concise; its program of proceedings is hardly more than three repetitions of one broadly tender melody. What brief and rudimentary second theme there is (beginning in the nineteenth measure) is closely related to the first, it will be noted, by the falling fourth of its accompaniment. It consists almost entirely of a few poignantly expressive double-stops for the violin, passionate in the high register, melancholy and dark in the low; and its function as second theme, which its brevity and casualness almost incline us to doubt, is corroborated by its recurrence, in the tonic, twenty-

five measures before the end, extended so as to lead with real
solemnity into the coda.

We are not surprised to find a mind imaginative enough to
make such an *Allegro* out of three motives and such an *Adagio*

Figure 73.

out of one theme needing for the lighter business of a scherzo none of the traditional properties of literal repetition and a separate trio, but on the contrary able to beat its whole texture from five saucy notes as a skillful *chef* beats a meringue from the white of an egg. These five notes may be seen at the beginning of Figure 73, a, the subject of the scherzo so appropriately marked *Un poco presto e con sentimento*; and it will be observed that although, curiously enough, they rise from the tonic to the minor third and descend to tonic again in the manner of the "tragic motives" we have examined, there is no more tragedy left in them than there is in a somewhat rueful smile, and that in fact the sleight of hand with which they are manipulated has almost, though not quite, dissipated their sentiment. If the interval of the minor third preserves the sentiment in spite of all, the whimsical division of the heavy beat into two *staccato* eighth-notes, and the coy return to them after the brief rise to the third, fully advertises that this interval is to be toyed with rather than taken seriously. The amusing way in which the twin notes later worm their way down to the C sharps with which our quotation ends, confirms this impression.

The only other motives used in the movement arise quite incidentally and casually out of this one of the twin notes as the comedy proceeds: notably a group of descending eighth-notes that the violin, in the eighteenth measure, augments from the fleet sixteenth-note groups of the piano, and, in the next measure, a more emphatic quarter moving to a half which, as the piano presently shows us, is in reality only the playful descending third turned earnest. This is literally the entire subject-matter of the six-page escapade, which for the rest covers all keys from the initial and final elvish F sharp minor to an almost pompous F minor and delicately pastoral F major, and all moods from the scatter-brained to the pensive.

Three or four brief glimpses of this kaleidoscopic comedy must suffice for our illustrations. First there is the theme itself, or a few measures of it (Figure 73, a): the twin notes delicately silhouetted in piano octaves, the violin laying in the harmonies in scarcely perceptible half-tone. Here the keynote of elvish playfulness is exactly struck. When the violin takes its turn at the twin notes the piano silhouettes a slightly more palpable figure, a descending scale. This passage is shown in skeleton only in 73, b. The "earnest" form of the descending third motive, coupled with the eighth-note figure, affords material for a passage of considerable sonority coming after the theme and as a foil for it. Then things quiet down, and in the innocence and pastoral peace of F major the first four measures of the theme are extended by the violin to six, with the three eighth-notes A, G, F making a coyly hesitant cadence (Figure 73, c). These three notes A, G, F, which in their original form, it will be remembered, were A, G sharp, F sharp, have in their new form provided the piano with its accompaniment figure. No wonder the imagination which has already made such rich play with them is not content to drop them with their cadence. In the continuation we find it changing first the A to A flat, then the G to G flat, and at last the whole group to equivalent notes (in the home key of F sharp minor) which neatly reintroduce the original theme for its recapitulation.

The last bits, to which Figure 74 is devoted, are only a whiff of the delicious coda—just enough to whet our appetite to play it all from the score. First there is the more restful form the violin now gives in double-stops to the twin acrobats who have played so many pranks for our pleasure. To it is appended the final whisk of the tail with which the piano, left hand, in five different octaves, outlines the descending scale it presented so much more sedately in 73, b. We should hardly expect the madcap fancy of this movement, however logically it sticks to its theme, to confine itself to any one register, or to stand on its dignity in getting from one to another.

In the finale, *Presto agitato*, whimsicality gives place to vigor, to an almost savage energy. There is something of Hungarian *elan* in this movement. Yet here too the playful element, especially in the many empty first beats of the

Figure 74.

rhythms, maintains itself amidst its more agitated surroundings. The economy of motives which has distinguished the preceding movements here takes the specific form of odd diminutions or shifts of rhythm, and even of a curious trickiness in putting the same motives in different parts of the phrase, and thus utilizing them to entirely different purpose. For example, in the main theme (Figure 75, a), the violin, *forte passionato*, swoops upon its three-note motive with insatiable energy; yet a moment later, in the bridge theme (75, b) which with its empty firsts is so far from being passionate that it is almost saucy, the same motive, simply by being transferred from the beginning to the middle of the phrase, becomes entirely subordinate.

Another unexpected rhythmic transformation overtakes parts of the second theme. In its pristine state (Figure 75, c) with its even-paced progress and its chorale-like harmonies,

Figure 75.

this is of earnest, not to say solemn expression. But in its cadences it undergoes a parcelling or shredding process, first into
groups of four notes, still even-paced (see 75, d) then into

groups of three, with an "empty first" where the first note should be, and at last (75, e) into a gliding headlong line of quick notes from which its original seriousness has quite evaporated.

When, towards the middle of the movement, we find the composer transforming the at first so passionate main theme into a quiet meditative song for the violin (75, f) with piano supplying the merest scaffolding of soft harmony on the off-beats, we conclude that his power to transform themes is now practically unlimited, and that his conjuration is so competent to draw any kind of a rabbit out of any kind of a silk hat that we may as well give up guessing as to what his themes will do next. Nevertheless a surprise or two still remain for us. After the long passage of persistent syncopation in which the two instruments seem to be constantly striving to unseat each other, but finally emerge (if they have luck) both triumphant in a proclamation of the theme in F minor, there commences, also in F minor, another excitingly rhythmic passage which sounds like the theme, yet somehow does not seem to be quite the theme after all. What is it? Examination reveals that the composer has been conjuring again and has made a new phrase from the soaring figure that appeared in the theme itself only as its cadence (Figure 75, a, measures 7 and 8). He is getting ready, in fact, for his coda, where, by another turn of the wrist this soaring figure is made to combine with the bridge motive (Figure 75, g). And then, half way through the coda, comes the last transformation scene (75, h). Here the second theme in the treble of the piano accompanies the first theme in the bass; whereupon the violin enters with the first theme in a chastened mood at last, its harmony now made rich and poignant instead of bold and clear. This dies away to *piano* and to a moment of pregnant silence before a fusillade of passionate chords whirl the movement to its end.

CHAPTER XX

THE VIOLA QUINTET IN G MAJOR, OPUS 111

THE second viola quintet occupies in the chamber music of Brahms a peculiar, in some ways a supreme place. With its immediate predecessor the D minor Violin Sonata it may be said to mark the high point of his achievement, the point after which, despite the mellow autumnal beauty of the Clarinet Quintet, the curve begins to descend. In all four of the works with clarinet one is conscious of a less buoyant, a more chastened mood, a sadder, more reflective beauty. Here on the other hand, in the work with which he himself had at first planned to close his creative life (before he was tempted by his friend Mühlfeld's clarinet to reopen it) he is at the height both of his technical powers and of his zest in life. Never before had he written at once with such mastery and such buoyancy of high spirits; even the D minor Sonata, though equally masterful, is less exuberant. The Quintet, product of the summer of 1890 at Ischl, and last expression of full and hearty manhood, is rich in invention even to prodigality. Well might his friend Frau Herzogenberg write him, in the fall of the same year: "He who can invent all this must be in a happy frame of mind! It is the work of a man of thirty."

The ferocious energy of the opening theme for the cello, the start of which is freely transcribed for piano in Figure 76, gave rise from the first to problems of interpretation. The upper players tended to get excited, and with their crowding accompaniment figures, in brilliant G major sonority, to drown

Theme I   Figure 76.

Allegro non troppo, ma con brio

Bridge:

out the cello entirely; doubt was felt whether any cellist less heroic than Hausmann, of the Joachim Quartet, would be able to make himself heard at all; and a sketch sheet, still in existence at the *Brahms Haus* in Gmunden, shows how Brahms tried inserting rests in alternation for the upper instruments. This was not of good effect, and the final decision was to damp down the violins and violas to *mezzo forte* with the entrance of the cello.

The adjustment needed, however, is quite as much one of tempi as of dynamics; the exciting effect of the opening figures tempts performers to play too fast as well as too loud. This is unfortunate for several reasons. First, too fast a tempo puts the cello player at a disadvantage, gives him time neither to sing his long notes nor to articulate his short ones. Second Brahms's music is always so complex in detail as to be confused if not played pretty deliberately; Franz Kneisel has recorded that it was difficult to play it deliberately enough to satisfy him. Third and most important of all, there is here involved the whole question of the unification of a sonata movement by uniformity of pace. With music so organic as Brahms's the vicious habit so many players have of racing every loud passage and dragging every soft one is simply disastrous. An improvisational style like Tschaikowsky's or Liszt's, in which a second theme often merely follows a first instead of following from it, may possibly survive such treatment; to Brahms destruction of continuity is fatal. Hence his tempi must all be considered together, and must essentially cohere, though with minor variations. In the present *Allegro non troppo* it will be found that if one will take a natural swing for the first half of the second theme (Figure 77) say about Metronome 60 for the dotted quarter, slightly accelerate it for the opening heroics of the cello, and slightly quieten it for the lovely *piano dolce* continuation of Theme II (Figure 78), one will hold the whole together and find it all clear, comfortable, and expressive.

The essential contrast embodied in the movement, of course, is that between the passionate ardor of the swinging cello-theme, with its athletic leaps, its rapid modulations, and its brilliant, full sonority, and the sensitive, almost shy tenderness of the two members of the other theme, so soft in their color-

Figure 77

ing, so reposeful in their harmonic sequences, so entrancing in their rhythmic hesitations. The wonder is, not merely how one mind can touch such extremes, but how it can manage to reconcile them within a rather concise form.

The vigorous leaps of the cello, forming in the second and

third measures a motive of a dotted eighth and three sixteenths used later as the condensed representative of the whole theme, soon disappear in favor of a rising third that begins to quiet their ardor as early as the sixth measure, and that motivates the whole passage commencing two measures further on, where our excerpt closes. Twelve measures later, at the "bridge" also shown in Figure 76 this third, now bold and passionate on the G-string of the second violin, has quite displaced the earlier groups, and begins to assume primary importance. At the same time a less conspicuous but equally significant change steals over the subordinate rhythm. The insistent sixteenth-notes give place to a swaying of eighths that in its quiet ease, verging on languor, suggests nothing so much as a distant Viennese waltz, or perhaps a pleasant country dance such as might voice the *dolce far niente* of the Prater Park of Vienna on a long summer afternoon. . . . Over this background now begin the lovely hesitant rises of the second theme (Figure 77) given in the sombre tone of the viola so dear to Brahms, and poising as if in question through the second and third beats, while the violins embroider the harmony. These hesitant rises, we notice, embody the rising third in a new form. And while we are quite aware that it is still subordinated both by its hidden position within the rhythmic group and by the sus-pensive harmonies that carry it, we also feel vividly its gradual transformation of the mood towards quiet tenderness. In the repetition by the ethereal tones of the violins, this tenderness touches the ecstatic.

It is only, however, in the still lovelier continuation of the theme, or "answer" (Figure 78) that the rising third at last comes into its own. Now it leaves all competing figures behind, and starting off each measure on the thesis of the rhythm, and in consonant chords that give it assurance and tranquillity, dominates the mood of peace. The caressing descents of a seventh which follow it mingle in this peace an ineffable wistful tenderness. All this is first presented, like the questioning half of the theme, in an undertone-color, this time the second violin,

Theme II.   Figure 78.

(Second strain - "Answer.")

and then, with childlike naïveté, immediately repeated by the violin, high and clear. Never has Viennese *gemüthlichkeit*, even in its supreme poets, Schubert and Brahms, reached a more perfect and touching expression than in this pair of naïve melodies, this expectant question and confident answer, in which happiness and sadness mingle as they always mingle in simple hearts. A music more innocent, more disarmingly unsophisticated, more homely and happy and human, one cannot imagine. Kalbeck tells us that he suggested for the quintet, at its rehearsal, the motto "Brahms in the Prater." "You've hit it," replied Brahms, with a twinkle in his eye: "Among the pretty girls."

The quiet mood is followed by a brief conclusion theme, full of busy agitation, completing the exposition; and then follows the development, highly complex, consisting of five contrasting sections. First comes a peaceful stretch, in which the rising third, emerging more saliently than ever, forms the entire material, rising dreamfully through various solo instruments over a murmurous accompaniment. The reappearance of the characteristic cello figure of the start marks the second section, embodying the more passionate elements in the drama. As this culminates in section three, a momentarily abortive attempt to recapitulate the main theme, the music quiets once more to *dolce* and a richly colored passage begins, with modulations to lush regions of tropical vegetation, so to speak, and the emergence of a new motive, in repeated eighth-notes, that seems to carry us into enchanted places. The same new motive then, in a final section, becomes more assertive *(forte ben marcato)*, and introduces a climax which soon leads to the real recapitulation. After the almost bewildering variety and dramatic energy of the development, its forthrightness is grateful.

The amplitude with which the whole movement is allowed to expand itself, in striking contrast with the laconic conciseness of the D minor Sonata, is especially evident in the coda. The conclusion theme, formerly so busy and so agitated, this time forgets its agitation and loses its busyness in a leisurely day-dream wherein its phrases wind about each other with all

the easy deliberation of the middle themes, and in a dallying
of tonic and dominant worthy of folk-song. Only for a moment does a phrase of the answering strain of the second
theme threaten, in G minor, a more troubled mood, which

Figure 79.

harmlessly smooths out into another quiet dominant-tonic
cadence, introducing the real point of the coda. This is nothing
less than the final confrontation and reconciliation of the two
elements whose opposition has created the drama. Figure 79
shows with what concentrating art the irrepressible cello theme
is now distilled to its most essential figure, over which the rising third, harmonized in simplest triads, with equal condensation symbolizes the softer element. This delicious retrospect
upon the now enacted drama seems in its simplicity to carry
us to the very springs of German folk-song. It merges into the
few measures of exuberant cadence, in the vein of the main
theme, that bring to completion one of the most magnificent
allegros in all chamber music.

The nobly tragic expression of the *Adagio* is due partly
to the theme itself (Figure 80, a), even more to its treatment,
without any "contrast", and with a concentration worthy of

Bach. First it appears, as in the figure, in D minor. Later
it is developed in G minor, and brought to a climax in the major
mode of the original key. At the end recurs the touching minor

form with a new and at once simpler and more poignant treatment of the continuation, as shown in Figure 80, b, the coda;
and at the very close it assumes a noble dark earnestness on
the lowest strings of all the instruments. And that is all.
"I find the *Adagio*," wrote Frau Herzogenberg to Brahms,
"superior to the C sharp minor movement of the earlier quintet in its unity and continuity of feeling. I am always rather
worried by middle parts, written in the spirit of contrast, but
here it is a case of mutual reflection and enhancement."

With the *Poco Allegretto* Brahms enters the world of
smiling half pensive humor, of innuendo, implication, half
hints, ambiguous suggestions, delicate disappointments and
unexpected realizations, in which his intermezzi live. How
are we to follow him into this world, of which he leaves the door
invitingly ajar? "The true business of the literary artist,"
says Stevenson, "is to plait or weave his meaning, involving
it around itself; so that each sentence, by successive phrases,
shall first come into a kind of knot, and then, after a moment
of suspended meaning, solve and clear itself." The theme of
the *Poco Allegretto* (Figure 81, a), looked at with this definition in mind, shows us not only how close kin are the two
time arts, music and literature, but also how much more complicated is this "plaiting or weaving" in music, where the interaction of rhythmic and tonal structures brings about such an
indescribable involution. Consider, for instance, abstracting for
simplicity the rhythmic from the tonal aspect, merely the
melody of the first eight measures. It falls, we see, into six
groups filling a pair of measures each, the first measure of each
pair heavy, the second light. But the note-groups themselves fall unevenly within these boundaries, often with highly
ingenious and beautiful effects: thus the little runs of three
eighth-notes do not belong to the group where they appear, but
are always "anacrustic" or preparatory to the next group, as our

brackets indicate. Each note-group becomes then a cluster
of two longer notes in feminine rhythm (moving from heavy
to light) with an anacrusis introducing the first; and each, up

Figure 81.

(Theme repeated.)

Figure 81. (continued.)

to and including the high G, "involves the meaning around itself," as Stevenson says, or ties the knot, which is then only untied by the last few groups. Finally, the last two groups are no longer feminine but masculine, giving a certain solidity to the cadence.

Now look at the melody. The two opening notes D, C sharp, with their curious wistful droop, set the motto of the whole. The D and C natural that follow vary it, give a nuance to its meaning that no man can describe, but all can feel. The G and F clinch it in gentle climax. The E flat and D abate the climax towards repose, or, in Stevenson's phrase, help "untie the knot." The long G, and still more the long D, complete the cadence.

Now take the harmony. At once we see how immensely it enhances the rhythmic and melodic beauties. Thus the D, C sharp motto really becomes completely itself only when the clear and consonant harmony of the D progresses into the trouble and tension of the C sharp: the knot is now tied a hundred times more effectually. Similarly in the sixth measure, the harmony produces a suspense that carries the melody with a new strength to its next member, beginning with the E flat. Finally the suspensive harmony of measures 9 to 12 counteracts any possible heaviness in the long cadencing notes G and D. In the repetition that immediately follows the melody shown in the figure, these cadencing long notes are reversed in function: tonic and dominant of G minor in the first half of this Part I are answered by dominant and tonic of D minor in the second half, completing the tune with a full cadence.

In Part II the anacrusis is reduced from three eighth-notes to a single quarter, and a new motive, D, F, leads off in violin, is imitated by viola, and ends by generating a four-measure phrase. The viola, with the same notes a step lower, C, E flat, answered by violin, generates a twin phrase. The natural sequence is then the same notes still one further step lower— B flat, D flat. But we are now made aware, by the doubling of the D flat in both of the outer, most prominent voices, by the cessation of all musical interest in the minor voices in favor of a mere background of syncopation, and above all by the constant harping upon the D flat, that something new is in the wind, or, to change the figure, that the cat is going to jump a new way this time. The cat is manifestly using that D flat as her platform for a new spring somewhere—but where?—that is what worries us! And then, all in a breath, the D flat suddenly changes to C sharp, and to a long note in a heavy measure, and by resolving up to D whisks us back from the remote key of B flat minor to our original G minor, and presents us with a motive (C sharp, D) that we recognize as the reversal of the D, C sharp with which we began. Quite evidently, this is the solution of the problem there propounded, the answer to the question there set: for in place of its move-

ment from clear harmony to obscure, we now find an emergence
from a troubled chord into an unequivocal tonic.

This is the high point of the whole piece, immediately repeated with a rhythmic expansion that increases its weightiness,
and that leads into some filigrees for violin in which the step
C sharp, D is once more glanced upon in a veiled reference.
Particularly beautiful are the cadences of the last eight bars.
Their essence is an expansion of the two bars of dominant and
two of tonic, which ended Part I, to four bars each. But within
this pattern there is room for a fascinating new reference to
the F sharp and C sharp neighbors of the tonic and dominant
tones, in a new motive of even quarters, and for a droll whimsy
of filling up the four bars of the final G with other things that
keep it from being quite final after all:—especially with a
breathless little pause followed by two soft major chords that
anticipate the brighter color of the trio.

This trio, with its debonair folk-theme set for alternating
pairs of violas and violins, sounds so innocent that we might
well suppose at first it had no particular bearing on anything
that went before. Study quickly dispels that impression. It has
both a melodic and a harmonic correspondence to the minor
theme, destined to delightful developments. The melodic
correspondence is that the tonic-dominant G, D which in Figure 81, a, made up the four-bar cadence, is here (81, b) echoed
and resumed in the two quarter-notes G, D that cadence the
viola phrase (repeated by the first violin). To this we shall
return. The harmonic correspondence is that, just as the whole
second part of the earlier tune was built around the musical
pun or play-upon-notes of insisting strongly on D flat and then
taking it as C sharp, neighbor to the dominant note D, so here
the whole second part plays with the F sharp that is the
neighbor of the tonic note G. Already in the first part, shown
in our Figure 81, b, this F sharp enters in the seventh measure,

in the bass, as the dominant of B minor. Two measures later it becomes the dominant of B major, and two later still, chameleon-like, it has become the leading tone of G once more, and leads us back to the repeat of the whole tune.

But it is in the second part that this chameleon F sharp begins to play tricks upon us. First it falls to F natural, and leads us (if we may follow its mischievous example and pun a little too) not *unnaturally* to expect it to respect this natural and keep on going down, to E and so on. But not at all! It no sooner persuades us to start downward than it doubles back to F sharp again, and while we are still wondering what that means, even "carries on" up to G. Here it stays a good while. "Ha, ha", we exclaim, "now we have it, it is going to C major." "Fooled again," cry all five voices at once with a truly portentous unison F sharp; "We said F sharp, and we mean it. We said dominant B minor, and we mean that. . . . Well, at any rate we mean F sharp, though perhaps it is leading tone of G major. . . . Well, come to think of it, the cello knows he means F sharp, but he is no longer quite sure what it is . . ." and while he is trying to find out, he has gone down through E to D, carried us back to our original key of G, and reluctantly surrenders the limelight to the gently gossiping pairs of violas and violins!

It is in the coda that the melodic correspondence we spoke of comes to its fruition. We remember that the second viola had in the trio two quarter-notes G, D, that resumed the half-cadence of the earlier tune. It was echoed by the violin, so that the whole tune ran along suspensively, without reaching a complete cadence—that was part of its charm. Now however (Figure 81, c) by simple inversion, this G–D, with its questioning half-cadence as if to say "Is it?"—becomes D–G, and says with some firmness, "It is." But wait: the violins, to which it is now given, are countered by the two violas, in the original

hrase with G–D—"Is it?" The rest of the gentle colloquy
an be read from our illustration as from a book. The give-and-
ake of interrogative and conclusive becomes quicker; every

Figure 82.

ime violin says "It is," viola demurs "Is it?"; and it is only
vhen the violin takes matters into its own hands, goes up to its
ighest G and stays there two full measures, that the decision
eems to be in favor of the affirmative. Yet after all, we are
ricked once more. At the end of the long arpeggio the violin

compromises, and climbs down to D; and the whole matter is left in pleasing uncertainty!

The gentle quizzing of the scherzo turns in the finale into downright broad humor. It is a most joyful piece. Its carefree main theme (Figure 82, a), elastic in rhythm, dancing in figuration, exuberantly insistent on tonic and dominant, is countered by a curiously sinuous tune (82, b), a veritable Irish jig. All sorts of merriment are made with the two tunes before the first, in a final *animato*, is bodily transformed into a wild Hungarian dance.

CHAPTER XXI

THE CLARINET TRIO, OPUS 114

AT the beginning of the nineties Brahms seems first to have felt the physical and mental languor of increasing age that reflected itself slowly but surely in the changing character of his art. Though it was in the summer of 1890 that he composed the buoyant G major Quintet, his friend Billroth, visiting him at Ischl in May, reported of him in a letter: "He rejected the idea that he is composing or will ever compose anything." This was no doubt a passing mood; but a year later we find Brahms himself saying: "I have tormented myself to no purpose lately, and till now I never had to do so at all; things always came easily to me." It was not to be sure until 1895 that actual physical disease betrayed itself in an unhealthy color; chronic invalidism was delayed until the fall of 1896, and death until April, 1897; but already in the early nineties Brahms's vigorous constitution was struggling against a sense of weariness unmistakably reflected in even the greatest of his works of these last years, the Clarinet Quintet. No doubt it was this unwonted weariness that made him wonder whether he had not better end his work with the G major Viola Quintet of 1890.

Had he done so his chamber music would have closed with one of its greatest masterpieces instead of with the graceful but less spontaneous clarinet sonatas. But on the other hand it would have lacked a whole group of works, the four with clarinet, which, whatever their deficiencies, constitute with their dark yet rich coloring, their concise though subjective thought, replacing the exuberant melodies of youth with pondering contrapuntal mutations of themes, austere frequently to the verge of bareness, and their melancholy, stoical, often tragic feeling, a department of his music that is unique.

The particular incitement to the composition of these last four works was Brahms's delight in the clarinet playing of his friend Richard Mühlfeld, of the Meiningen Orchestra, whom he considered the greatest player on any wind instrument known to him. The clarinet, mingling better with the piano, as Brahms thought, than the bowed instruments, is no less romantic in expression and luscious in tone-color than the horn, while far more various in tone and flexible in articulation. It rivals indeed the violin in the variety of its tone-color in different registers (if not quite in intimate human feeling in its expression), and equals the piano in flexibility, adding a certain indescribable sort of voluble neatness peculiar to itself. It has three separate registers, each strongly characterized and each appealing potently to the musical nature of the mature Brahms. Its upper register is a clear and lyric soprano, slightly less sensitive than that of the violin but of an incomparable roundness and clarity. The middle register has a sort of mysterious hollowness, a sighing softness that Brahms uses *con amore.* Above all, the lower register, the so-called "chalumeau," is dark, sober, even menacing at times, in a degree equalled by no other instrument; and as Niemann well says: "With Brahms, the later the work the more sombre the color." Finally the extraordinary flexibility and smoothness of utterance peculiar to this instrument make available not only such impassioned gipsy-like recitatives as those of the *Adagio* of the Quintet, but the neat dovetailing of intricate figuration between piano and clarinet so fascinating in the finale of the E flat Sonata.

No wonder the clarinet opened to Brahms what is virtually a new vein in his genius.

Despite the fact that the Trio is the weakest of the four works with clarinet, and indeed one of the weakest of all his works, constituting a deep trough between the two crests of the Viola Quintet and the Clarinet Quintet, its opening *Allegro* reveals quite clearly what the peculiar qualities of this new vein are to be. Indeed, so concentrated is now his style and personal feeling that the dozen measures of the opening theme alone (Figure 83, I a) afford us a true sample of the whole. The mood is serious and sombre, permeated by a sadness that dictates a minor mode, a monotonous bass with slow syncopations, and a theme reverting, as so many of the later themes do, to the tragic formula of effortful rise from the key-note and weary re-descent thereto. The clarinet tone-color is beautifully used to support and intensify this mood. Its clear, pleading high notes in its opening phrases quickly give place to the hollow tones of the chalumeau, and it ends the theme with a sigh on its lowest C sharp and the neighboring E. (Brahms is obliged to use the A clarinet instead of the more usual and easily manageable B flat instrument, in order to get this low C sharp.)

Despite the gloomy luxury of the coloring, the theme itself unfortunately lacks the vitality of such a theme as opens, say, the third violin sonata (albeit that is minor and tragic, too). There is here a sort of poverty, or perhaps intentional bareness, of line that is only dissembled by the sequence the clarinet makes to the cello phrase, or by the threes to a beat that vary its rhythm almost manneristically. In the rhythmically more energetic motive (83, I b) that follows and complements this first period, a rather schematic use is made, as in many of the themes from now on, of inversion. Its second half, instead of being currently invented, imitates the first by literal inversion, a

contrapuntal device valuable to unity but apt to be dangerous to the impression of spontaneity. In the second theme also, shown in the figure only in melodic outline, it will be seen that there is resort to an almost mechanical inversion. The conclusion theme, in two strains, is hardly more felicitous as melody: the first strain, III a, is in a rather fretfully chromatic vein that contrasts painfully with so many diatonic tunes as clear as folk-song; the second, III b, is chiefly made of those successive descents of thirds that from about the time of the Fourth Symphony tend to become manneristic. Thus on the whole our impression of the themes is a disappointing one; they seem to betray an unmistakable apathy of the imagination.

If, unwilling to generalize from a single movement, we compare the other chief themes of the trio, our unhappy impression is on the whole corroborated. The main theme of the *Adagio* (Figure 84, a), despite its forthrightness of expression, is in the end somehow tame, somehow lacking in persuasive charm. We respect but do not love it. The widespread harmonies of its third measure, as characteristic as the similar ones in the very first *Adagio* we examined (see Figure 3) lack the hypnotic power of those, and fall a little bare. What is more serious, the rhythmic structure lacks the usual rich Brahmsian variety, tending to harden into pattern figures repeated literally (here a quarter-note tied to the first of four sixteenths.) This automatism is frequent enough in composers like Schumann or Tschaikowsky in their weaker moments, and is even not incompatible with lyric charm; but minds capable of the organic structure of Bach's air for the G-string, or the opening theme of Beethoven's A major Cello Sonata, or innumerable themes we have examined in this book, lapse into it only in moments of depressed vitality. The fact that we find it again in the bridge of the finale (Figure 85), different as that is in movement and feeling, is ominous.

In the *Andantino grazioso*, in some ways the most attractive movement of the four, we find ourselves obliged to make just the opposite criticism of the theme. This tune (Figure 84, b), far from being severe, is tuneful to triviality and of a charm so superficial that a few hearings of it bring satiety. It has an almost Italian sinuousness of line and suavity of manner that hardly becomes Northern art. Fuller-Maitland, one of

Figure 84.

the most enthusiastic and at the same time discriminating of Brahmsians, compares it with the theme of the E flat Clarinet Sonata for a certain *morbidezza*, "a beauty of such ripeness that the slightest touch must make it over-ripe," and says without mincing matters that it "comes very near to the borders of the commonplace," that "Balfe himself might have written something very like it," and that it is "the only instance in Brahms's music of want of distinction." Alas, compared with the exquisite simplicity of so many of the intermezzi, this over-dressed tune is like the pretty peasant maiden who has spoiled herself, for a holiday at the fair, with finery and cosmetics.

The main themes of the finale, shown in Figure 85, complete the story, and clinch the impression. Theme III is merely rather monotonous and trivial, with a tendency to the rhythmic patterns already noted in the bridge. But I and II are more symptomatic of the abeyance of the imagination, fortunately momentary, in which this work was written. For is it not evident that their restless changes of meter, from 2–4 to 6–8, and from 6–8 to 9–8, are prompted by the uneasy sense in the composer's own mind of the monotony of his themes, and of the desirability of varying them at all costs? Now when his mind is at its full power it is magnificently capable of getting all necessary variety by rhythmic change, on a basis of uniform meter. His plastic powers are so great that he resorts much less frequently than less imaginative composers to metrical experiments like the 3–4, 2–4 of the Opus 101 Trio, being able to fill the commonest measures with endless rhythmic beauty. The rather pointless changes of meter we find here, then, are a sign not of rhythmic vitality, but of defective rhythmic control. The analogy is close between such metric restlessness and the kind of harmonic restlessness that finds expression in constant purposeless modulation. It is not, as is sometimes believed, the imaginative composer who modulates, or changes

Figure 85.

his time-signature, at every bar; it is on the contrary the unim-
aginative one, who thus reveals his poverty of thought in an
itch for surface effect. Hence the metrical fussiness here shown
is another evidence that when Brahms wrote this trio he was

for some reason temporarily but definitely below par in thematic inventiveness.

Even in his greatest works, however, we must remember, the greatness has been less apparent in the themes themselves than in what he does with them. Throughout this book we have had a growing sense of the miracles possible to his creative imagination—of the way no melody is static and fixed to him as to less genial minds, but the most unpromising motives flower into beauty as bare winter branches burgeon in the spring sun. Is this transmuting warmth, we must ask ourselves, operative here? If it is, the bareness of the twigs on which it works need not trouble us.

Unfortunately the answer must again be preponderantly negative. Except in the first movement there is comparatively little germination of thought: the themes are apt, as with less imaginative composers, to remain in the coda much what they were in the exposition. The coda of the slow movement, for instance, is disappointingly literal in comparison with such a re-creation as that in so early a work as the A major Piano Quartet. The only notable transformation the theme undergoes here is a very beautiful simplification of its melodic line the second time it is presented in full by the clarinet. The *Andantino* presents comparatively little opportunity for development; but it is disquieting to find in its coda, *Un poco sostenuto*, those almost mechanical repetitions of a brief motive, placed in a three-beat measure so as to take cross accents, which tend in late Brahms to degenerate into a mannerism.

In the finale, the most disappointing of all the movements in the themes themselves, the impression of formulism in their treatment is also most unescapable. When the clarinet takes up the second theme immediately after the cello has presented it, the cello follows along (it is this version that we have shown in our illustration, Figure 85, II) with the same melody, *in strict canon, after one beat, by inversion.* It takes no doubt a master of counterpoint to do this sort of thing, but after it is done it sounds more like a contrapuntal exercise than a human tune. In another passage the clarinet starts that sort of progression by downward thirds which tended to become manneristic in late Brahms, and does not stop until it has traversed literally twenty-three notes thus descending in thirds, finally landing on its lowest E (sounding C sharp). Such things savor more of routine than of spontaneity.

It is odd to see how the critics have all felt themselves repelled by this school-masterish, pedantic side of Brahms (let us say it boldly) exposed rather pitilessly by the Trio because of its lack of inspiration. Few of them meet the situation with Florence May's refreshing frankness, pronouncing this "one of the least convincing of his works." Colles contents himself with saying it sounds like a study for the instrument, Fuller-Maitland with pointing out a commonplace theme. A recent very sympathetic critic, Henry S. Drinker, Jr., in an attractive small guide to "The Chamber Music of Johannes Brahms", notes the peculiarities, but seems to like them. "The last movement," he says, "is full of startling and most interesting rhythmic changes" (are these changes, metrical rather than rhythmic, at all startling or particularly interesting?) "and contains one of his characteristic themes descending in intervals of a third, here for sixteen successive notes." (We should make the score 23 rather than 16, but we should hesitate to consider the theme "characteristic" of anything but the least treasurable side of Brahms.)

The most amusing unconscious confession of involuntary repulsion from the finale is found in Fuller-Maitland's book. He starts in boldly: "The finale is in a mixture of 2–4 and 6–8 time, such as Brahms loved," and then, evidently after a further look at the score, finds his heart fail him, and without making a new paragraph, or even starting a new sentence, presses on with: "But the whole trio has suffered by the simultaneous publication of one of the loveliest of all the master's works, the quintet for clarinet and strings," etc., etc. . . . A distaste that can thus upset the equanimity of so friendly a critic and dismantle the composition of so able a writer must be formidable indeed. Every Homer has a right to nod occasionally; but it seems to be the unspoken consensus that in this finale Brahms nods as industriously as a Chinese figurine.

Figure 86.

The exception that proves, or at any rate illuminates, the rule is found in the first movement. Here truly creative use is made of so simple an element as a rippling scale of sixteenth-notes, and with it the closing page is made murmurous. More fundamentally, the second strain of the main theme, (Figure 83, I, b) is gradually, as the movement proceeds, transformed from its initial energy into a more and more grave expressiveness. Already in the development, its restless triplets changed to slow-moving quarter-notes, it gives rise to a solemn antiphony between clarinet with cello in hollow octaves, and piano in chords. In the coda, in the passage shown in Figure 86, it takes on all the noble severity that is in last analysis the unique note of this uneven work. Listen to the new poignancy of expression it gets as clarinet and cello move in tenths instead of octaves; hear how in waning energy it seems to halt, first reduced to three notes, finally to two; and then feel the mystery of its final presentation, by the solo instruments, breathing the softest *pianissimo* two octaves apart. All this is instinct with the melancholy so typical of these last works with clarinet; and it is presented with an unrelenting seriousness in striking contrast to the radiant charm with which it is tempered in the Quintet. There the shadows are like those we see on snow in a day of blue sky—tinged, whatever their darkness, with lustrous cobalt. Here sky as well as earth is gray; charm is not offered, it is not even expected or desired. In recompense for its absence we find a high, unyielding sincerity, a grave dignity, a kind of stoic Roman virtue.

CHAPTER XXII

THE CLARINET QUINTET, OPUS 115

THE two essential powers of Brahms's genius, the power to conceive elements of a simplicity that give them universality, and the power to evoke from them an undreamed richness of meaning, reach in the Clarinet Quintet their incomparable perfection. The essential simplicity of the material is illustrated in Figure 87, showing the main theme of the first movement in full, and in Figure 88, the first and more striking half of the second theme. In all this rich play of music there are only three or four root ideas.

First there are those pleading, crying thirds and sixths of the two opening measures, circling in sixteenth-notes round the longer chords, making up what for convenience of reference we may call the "circling motive." One reason for the poignancy of this motive is possibly its tonal ambiguity, its uncertain hovering between D major and B minor as a lost soul might hover between earth and heaven. Its rhythm and coloring also add greatly to its expressiveness. The same tonal uncertainty continues through the third and fourth measures, where we hear twice a highly sensitive, a hauntingly beautiful motive, which we may identify as the "dipping motive" because it dips to the chromatic neighboring notes of its essential tones, B in its first measure, F sharp in its second. These essential notes are the tonic and the dominant tones of the key of B minor, thus embodying that tonic-dominant relation which to Brahms is always structurally supreme.

Figure 87

The essential motive of the second theme, on the other hand, grows not out of the chord, but out of the scale. Its first three notes, G, F sharp, E, (see Figure 88), immediately repeated as F sharp, E, D, give rise by inversion to the six freer notes that complete the first phrase. A deeper opposition between the themes than their melodic motivation is their rhythm: the first is thetic—both its motives begin on the heavy beat; the second owes much of its urgency to its start on the anacrustic sixth beat, maintained throughout. Curious for the thoroughness with which it mediates between these two central contrasting ideas is the highly concise bridge (the last three measures of Figure 87). Its opening measure is a highly vigorous form of the B, F sharp (tonic-dominant) that was announced covertly in the third and fourth measures. In its next measure, after a striking "empty first", it sounds at once the three notes in scale-line, the first an anacrusis (made more boldly unmistakable by being shortened to a sixteenth) necessary to prepare the second theme. These three potent measures thus resume the essential in Theme I and anticipate the essential in Theme II.

But the real wonder begins when we study the intricate fabric woven from these simple strands. The first theme, beginning in tentative, almost improvisational style, gets fully under way only at the eighteenth measure—it is there that we find the first tonic chord of B minor, in root position, on a heavy beat. Much of the tenderness of the theme may be traced to this shy, hesitant manner of its starting. The clarinet enters, at the fifth measure, in D major, impressively but ambiguously (since the tonality is to be B minor) with a slow upward arpeggio landing on high F sharp. Here it twice sounds the "circling motive", now doubled in length by that process of holding up a theme on a single note we first observed in the Horn Trio,—a process never more happily used than here, where it is so potently aided by the beautiful natural *crescendo-diminuendo* of the clarinet. A short cadenza leads to a form of the "dipping motive," eloquent in cello and viola, that is modified so as to rise to the higher F sharp instead of falling to the lower, and at the same time given its definitive form. It is this more assertive form that now, in the eighteenth measure, finally announces, in a quietly impassioned cantilena for the two violins, the main subject of the movement. Notice how in the fourth measure of this the earlier half-cadence B, F sharp takes the conclusive form F sharp, B. Despite the melodic elaboration that somewhat covers these central tones, they are clearly perceived as the armature of the cadence; and even more strongly do they dominate its augmented repetition, which leads directly to the bridge. Thus the whole theme is shaped by this antithesis, later to become still more significant, between the inconclusive cadence Tonic-dominant in its fourth measure and this final, strong Dominant-tonic.

The second theme again is a marvel of the expressive moulding of simple materials. Its earnest diatonic melody is started in D major by the clarinet, the second half phrase answering in violin. At measure 7 of Figure 88 the violin resumes the melody in more florid and intense form. By measure 11 we feel a diminution of force, a darkening of atmosphere, as the theme carries us to the successive subdominant keys of G and C, where, the rhythm also dying down, there comes a mysterious moment of waiting, a sort of ominous pause, the violin only reminding us with four notes that the theme is not forgotten. This is a remarkable instance of the momentary darkening of musical atmosphere by the use of keys on the subdominant side, with simultaneous rhythmic abatement; in the brightening that presently compensates it we move as imperceptibly back to D major. The four notes breathed out by the clarinet in its tenderest tones start a *crescendo*, and the theme itself soon returns, sounded *forte* and with intense passion by high clarinet, its original anacrusis of one eighth-note multiplied in length by five (measure 20). With this brave assertion of the initial motive, once more back in its

Figure 88.

original key, our figure must close; but the more we examine the theme thus shown in its essential outlines the more nearly incredible will seem the imagination that can evoke such varied beauty from three notes of the scale.

The development begins with the "circling motive" of sixteenth-notes, first quietly treated in the bass, then penetrating through the whole texture and rising to the mood of restless agitation. Suddenly this motion stops, and in D flat major, *quasi sostenuto*, the bridge theme enters, deeply impressive in its severe harmonies and its solemn pauses. The rhythmic figure of its second measure, three equal eighth-notes preceded by an anacrustic sixteenth, becomes more and more insistent. The key changes, to B flat, to D flat, to A major, to F, to C; always the rhythmic figure, often in bass, becomes more relentless, more inescapable. Finally, as F sharp is reached, the dominant of the original key, there is a hush, a pause, and the motive, its initial sixteenth quieted to an eighth, sounds ruminatingly in the lowest notes of the cello. With equal mystery the clarinet answers, in dark chalumeau notes, with its *inversion*. The cello repeats it; violin answers with the inversion. The cello cedes, falls back a step but repeats it lower, beginning on E; upper instruments answer with the inversion, reducing the four notes to three, as does the cello in its answer. Thus return, as if in a dream, the original key, tempo, and mood, and at last the main theme itself in recapitulation.

The apotheosis of the first theme, recorded in Figure 89, is reserved for the coda, one of the most deeply tragic and impressive ever conceived by Brahms. The final note, in keeping with the underlying mood of the whole work, is to be one of stoic acceptance of tragedy, of noble resignation. But this is to come only after the abatement of a crisis of impassioned grief; and it is with this that the coda, and our figure, commence. The circling motive, cried out *forte* in the high register of the two chief protagonists of the drama, the clarinet and the first violin, starts from the same note, F sharp, as at first, but instead of resting statically on the tonic of B minor is now launched energetically from the active dominant harmony of

E minor. In the same way the harmonic changes of the dipping motive give it a new plangency and headlong impetuosity.
In the fifth measure the circling motive is made shorter (half
a measure instead of a whole one) and proportionately more
vigorous; in the ninth it goes into the bass, still in the same
truncated impatient form.

But now begins the abatement. The bass motive gradually
loses energy and changes to rising arpeggios, in cello, then
viola, then violin, leading at last to the same plaintive, pathetic
third, F sharp–D, with which the piece began. From this point,
twelve measures from the end, every detail is significant. First
the circling motive is heard twice, exactly as at first (but with
how immeasurably heightened a pathos, after the passion that
has but just died away!) The dipping motive, too, in its
weariness exchanges the original restless syncopations of its
bass for slower, heavier ones, and stretches itself out to three
measures by pausing on its last *pianissimo* chord. Clarinet alone
now starts the dipping motive, in a new rhythmic form of in-
finite sadness, its first two notes anacrustic, its upward-resolv-
ing note (the A sharp) coinciding with a heavy measure, to
which even greater weight is given by the entrance with it of
full harmony. After a silence on the first half of the weak
measure in this block of two, the clarinet again sighs out A
and G as a new anacrusis, and on the heavy measure of a new
block of six (the final *fermata* being equivalent to one measure)
it reaches an indescribably poignant E sharp resolving up to
F sharp. This E sharp owes its poignancy not only to its
melodic position as under-neighbor to the dominant tone, but
to its rhythmic post on the heavy measure, and above all to its
harmonization with the second inversion of the tonic chord,
with fifth in bass, which lays upon it a burden, as of dumb
suffering, almost unbearable. And now comes, as last word,
the completion of the B, F sharp of the start with the F sharp,

Figure 89.

B which in the hollow tones of the clarinet, all alone, sound a pronouncement of doom. Almost unbelievable is the tragedy concentrated in those two unaccompanied notes. As they die away, two grave minor chords write *finis*.

It may seem strange to call a movement as sad as the *Adagio* a relief; yet there is so divine a tenderness in it, with its timidly smiling B major and its caressing three-beat metres, that it has the effect of relief after the stoicism, sometimes passionate and sometimes despairing, of the *Allegro*.

The first of its three parts is devoted to the B major song breathed forth by the clarinet, answered with a quietude even more intense by the violin, and finally summed up by both together in their most pleading tones. The first two times the G major chord marks and clinches the acme of the phrase, with its poignant dissonance smoothing out into the dominant F sharp chord. The last time this G major is exchanged for the even more poignant C major, similarly melting into the complete tonic, B. The contrast section here is of an exalted simplicity. Beginning at the *piano dolce*, it develops briefly the melody of the preceding cadence, the violins singing high and clear against the quiet background. As this ends, an upward run of the clarinet takes it to the very F sharp where it began; but instead of starting the theme again it sounds a changed version of it, four notes instead of three, harmonized to keep all in suspense, poised and mystical. Three times it starts, in descending keys, and, since it is a four-beat motive in a three-beat measure, successively on later beats. It poises a moment as if uncertain—and resumes the theme. The whole contrast is touching in its child-like candor.

Part II, the famous Hungarian-like middle section, marked *Più lento*, grows, like almost everything in the movement, out of the three notes of the opening measure. Its florid clarinet phrases, shown at Figure 90, b, stripped of their ornamentation

a. Adagio.　Figure 90.

b. Piu lento.

c.

read B, G, F sharp, and D, B, A. In treatment this section is as rhapsodic as the first is concise and spare. Its modulations become more and more colorful; its figurations grow ever faster, fuller, and more furious; towards its end, leaps from one extreme to the other of the register of the clarinet suggest an almost mad frenzy of improvisation. It is one of the richest realizations in the chamber works of the spirit of Gipsy music that we noted as early as the "Rondo alla Zingarese" of the G minor Piano Quartet.

After the B major song has been repeated in a Part III almost exactly like Part I, there is a brief, touchingly simple coda in which a phrase of ethereal gentleness is sung by the clarinet (Figure 90, c) and repeated at once, slightly expanded, in the more troubled tones of the violin G-string. What is this phrase, so unerringly reaching our hearts, so familiar and yet so full of a resignation sadder even than any we have yet heard? It is, we see, just the opening phrase, F sharp, D sharp, C sharp—each of its notes augmented to dominate a whole measure, and given movement by an arabesque of subordinate notes. Could anything be simpler?—and could anything less simple be so infinitely touching? And finally even the cadence confesses the domination of the theme; for it consists of the first two notes of it only, F sharp, D sharp, breathed forth by the clarinet in a last dying sigh.

"This dialogue between the violin and the clarinet," records Fuller-Maitland, "cannot be forgotten by any who had the happiness of hearing the Quintet interpreted with Joachim and Mühlfeld in these parts." "The clarinetist," he says, "seemed to express in the *pianissimo* phrase the inmost secrets of the human heart in a mood of passionate rapture; one thought, as he played, that the smallest touch more must end in exaggeration; yet when Joachim took up the phrase he put even more into it than Mühlfeld had done, and yet kept it entirely within the picture and within the bounds of truest art." Florence May describes one of the early performances by the same players, at which Brahms was present. "My place," she writes, "was only two or three away from his, and so situated that I could see him all the time the work was being played. His face wore an unconscious smile, and his expression was one of absorbed felicity from beginning to end of the performance." Brahms, one realizes, was as happy in his interpreters as they were in having such music to play.

The *Andantino* is the last example in the chamber music of that type of light movement in which a lyric section is contrasted with a deft *presto* or *vivace*, usually with some interrelation of pace between the two, sometimes with actual thematic resemblance. In this case we find both, with also an experiment, rather unusual, in the exact equivalence of the cadences of the two sections. The *staccato* motive of the *Presto non assai*, with its amusing harping on D, is merely a fleet and whimsical variant of the four notes that open the *Andantino* in a graceful *legato*, while the dancing pairs of chords that accompany it is derived from another incidental theme in the *Andantino*. Thus all the material is shared by the two sections in common, silhouetted in the one against D major, in the other against B minor. The two sections are contrasted not only thus quaintly in key, but more fundamentally in their structure. The *Andantino* is brief, is all in D major without modulation, and presents nothing but the motive, a slight contrast, and a rather striking dying-away conclusion in which the motive fades out against a background of long-held D's. The *Presto*, on the other hand, carried through with an irrepressible flow of fancy, is a complete little rondo, in B minor, kept bubbling and dancing almost throughout by those *staccato* sixteenths prancing about their D. Curious is the effect of making the *Presto* end with the same dying-away against held D's as the *Andantino*,—the same though notated in measures half as long. We seem to have come full circle, and to end with a sense of essential reconciliation between the grace of the one tempo and the pranks of the other, already latent perhaps in their metrical relationship.

In the finale Brahms returns to the use of a structural device, an adaptation of cyclism, that he had tried out tentatively in the B flat Quartet, and used with deep imaginative beauty in the Third Symphony: the return at the end of the work to the theme with which it opened. In the quartet the effect has much charm, if no great profundity. In the symphony it gives a sort of retrospective glow to the closing page, it is less exciting than serenely lovely. Here, owing perhaps quite as much to the innocent naïveté of the finale theme proper and of its variations as to the profound sadness of the chief subject, it is overwhelmingly tragic in effect. In Figure 91 we see the variation theme in its pristine charm. Five variations follow, the first beginning as a cello solo, the fourth a delightful change from minor to major, and the fifth substituting the more graceful triple time for the duple so far used. With this subtle change (simultaneous with a return to minor) and with the infusion of a wistful pathos, we begin to feel something ominous in the atmosphere, a sense of change casting its shadow before it. As the bass begins its pulsing at the *Poco meno mosso*, therefore, we are prepared to return to the mood of the first movement—we feel, so to speak, that the sun is set, and that we wait only for night.

Wonderful is the passage, transcribed for piano in Figure 92, with which the whole work closes,—wonderful the art with which it combines the most significant features both of the variation theme and of the first movement. Its first four measures, reproducing the four which commenced the *Allegro*, so change their orientation as to start now not from the tonic but from the subdominant, profiting to the full by its sense of completion,

Figure 91.

and to reach, not D major opening out to new activities, but C major as a Neapolitan sixth weighty with the sense of cadence back to B minor. The rhythm is at the same time made to poise, much as it did near the end of the first movement, on the last note of the dipping motive, extending it implicitly through an extra measure of silence. As an unexpected answer to this question and pause comes a solemn unison, A sharp, B, in three octaves, imitating the D sharp, E. Extraordinary in its manifold bearing on the musical drama now drawing to its close is this mysterious A sharp, B. First of all, while thematically it is of course simply the dip from the second of the two chief motives of the *Allegro*, it is given now for the first time the rhythmic value of a full measure, heavy and light beat, which it did not have even when it appeared so impressively at the similar closing passage of that *Allegro*. In other words, it here receives its final rhythmic transfiguration, and rises to its highest possible emotional power. Secondly, it serves an important harmonic purpose in inflecting the subdominant towards the tonic, in preparation for the dominant to follow. Thirdly, by anticipation it prepares the bass of the following measure, E sharp, F sharp, where it is to serve as counter-subject to a touching cadence generated from the opening of the variation theme, and thus to aid that synthesis of the two themes which makes this coda the culmination of the whole work. As a glance at the Eulenberg score will show, this cadence is so divided that the clarinet almost timidly proposes the first *piano* measure of it, while the violin completes it with a passionate *forte;* and in the repetition the antithesis is even more dramatic, the clarinet breathing its first measure in even softer tones, the violin answering with even higher passion, and the clarinet continuing with a cadenza which takes it to its highest notes, uttered with maximum intensity.

As the cadenza dies away, the dipping motive takes the last word. Twice its original length, it is now so placed that its last two notes fill, as in the solemn unison, a full measure, heavy beat for the dissonant neighboring note, light beat for its resolution. But the cadence so formed is not only thus feminine

Figure 92.

in its rhythm within the measure; it falls also in a light or weak measure, thus taking an air of weakness, we might almost say brokenness, deeply touching. When, therefore, in its repetition still lower, its weak measure receives the same notes,

E sharp, F sharp, that at the end of the *Allegro* were already so moving, they take on an impression of fatality almost overpowering.

Nothing now remains but the F sharp, B (Dominant-tonic) completing the cycle; yet even this is immensely deeper in its pathos through an augmentation that holds its F sharp through two full measures. At last, as if unable to postpone the inevitable descent longer, the clarinet sinks to the B, unaccompanied as before; but the two chords that again close the movement are no longer merely solemn and soft: the first, *forte*, is a cry of despair; the second is the final acquiescence.

A pupil of Clara Schumann has described a meeting at the house of Kneisel in Ischl, where the Quintet was played by Mühlfeld and the Kneisel Quartet for Brahms and a few friends including Steinbach and Nikisch. "When they had finished playing this heavenly work," she says, "we were all so moved that nobody found a word to say. But Nikisch fell on his knees before Brahms, and that exactly expressed our feelings." It was a whimsical expression of a reverence that every music-lover must feel for the noble mind and the simple heart that could make this music.

CHAPTER XXIII

THE CLARINET SONATA IN F MINOR, OPUS 120, NO. 1

In the main theme of the F minor Sonata, the more sombre in mood of the two clarinet sonatas, we find a new variant of that "tragic motive" of which we have come upon so many examples. In its first estate, sounded in hollow three-octave unisons by the piano (Figure 93, I a), it is essentially a rise from the fifth, C, to F, followed by a slow descent to low F, made the heavier and sadder by the lowering of G, the second, to G flat. In its final form, in the coda, also shown in the figure, it approaches even more nearly the formula. It rises there on the piano from F, the tonic, to C at one leap, and slowly settles back again; the clarinet somewhat lightens its gloom by resuming briefly the original form and ending on the fifth, C, to which the change of harmony to major gives a sort of tender hopefulness. In the second measure of this theme may be noted the slow turn around D flat; it comes later to assume considerable importance. With this chief motive, shaped from the descending scale, is associated another and bolder one, given to the clarinet (I, b in Figure 93), moving through chord instead of scale line, and by those wide jumps in which the clarinet is so happy. After all this has been contrasted by more vigorous rhythms (measures 12–24) the chord motive returns in *forte*, tossed from piano to clarinet.

Like the first theme, the second is formed of two contrasting associates. The first is the quiet section shown in

Figure 93.

Figure 94, a; it is in D flat, emphasizing its seriousness by the excursion to the subdominant side; and it is a curious instance of the polyphonic methods of thought of the "last manner", as the first four notes of its bass are made from those of the first theme by augmentation, while from the chord motive of the same theme comes also the upward motive of the clarinet in its third measure. Here is economy of material with a vengeance. The second section, in the dominant, C minor, contrasts strongly with the first by its restless rhythm (Figure 94, b). This scanty material is turned to good account. The motives of the first two bars give rise to the striking augmentation shown at 94, c. The descending scale figure of five notes in

Figure 94.

the fourth measure, reappearing from the first theme, is presently augmented from eighth to quarter-notes, and provides the subject for an ingenious canonic passage between the two instruments. A short but emphatic concluding theme completes the exposition.

About a page of the development is concerned with the

quiet section of the second theme, providing a restful background for the piano against which the clarinet outlines gentle arabesques. As it proceeds, the turn to which attention was called in the second measure of the opening theme becomes more and more central, appearing in all voices in delightfully neat dovetailing. Another page is devoted to more stormy moods, both from the first theme and from the more dramatic and rhythmically active part of the second one shown in Figure 94, b.

After recapitulation of all themes comes a rather subjective and unexciting, but ripely meditated coda, *Sostenuto ed espressivo*. Here we find the final flowering of the chord-line motive of 93, I, b, allowed to generate a five-bar phrase, quite uneventful but full of the covert, almost repressed beauty characteristic of late Brahms. A short-hand version of it is shown in Figure 93, in which the right hand may play the melody, and the left the accompanying chords. Its repetition, slightly expanded, leads into the solemn final form of the opening theme already described.

The uneventfulness of the last manner, akin to Beethoven's absorbed day-dreaming in his last quartets, is balm to the spirit again in the beautiful *Andante un poco Adagio*. Whether for the simplicity and homogeneity of its form, based entirely on a single theme and using only incidental contrast, or for the gracious curves of its melody, or for the purity of its part-writing and its exquisite use of the lyric powers of the clarinet, this is one of the most intimately lovely of all the slow movements. The caressing tune is first presented by the clarinet, in A flat major, in its most lyric tones, against a soft background for the piano, so contrived that the basses complete the chord only on the weak rhythmic halves of the measures or beats. The result is a peculiar hesitant timidity of expression (see Figure 95, a). At the completion of this tune comes in the

piano, as casual contrast, a passage of graceful figuration, **very**
quiet, in the subdominant D flat, and made from the first three
notes of the tune by diminution. Is it to be a new theme, or

Figure 95.

only a contrast within the old one? The whole texture is so
unsalient we hardly know; but it soon loses itself in references
by the piano to the main theme, first in E, later in C, forming
a sort of middle part to the movement, closely related to be-

ginning and end. The theme now returns in the original A flat, first in the dark chalumeau register, but repeated in all its initial clarity. A very brief reminiscence of the casual contrast figuration ushers in a final condensed version of the tune, with *pianissimo* subdominant harmony, high in the piano. This is so reproduced in Figure 95, b as to be available to complete 95, a. In this whole movement there is nothing louder than the *poco forte* with which it commences; most of it is *pianissimo*, to be played *una corda* by the piano and with that merest whisper of softest tone for which the clarinet is so incomparable; it is like a meditation in the solitude of evening.

With the *Allegretto grazioso* returns animation—but a gentle animation, as in most of the Brahmsian intermezzi. Some of the curves of this delightful tune (the opening phrases are shown in Figure 96, a) with their chromatic grace, have almost the touch of *morbidezza* deplored by Fuller-Maitland in the Trio—but not quite; on the whole it is as strong as it is graceful. There is a tireless freshness of impulse about the way it constantly renews itself; and when, after the rhythmic augmentation with which the contrast pauses, the tune returns in the piano, against contented burblings from the clarinet, and the clarinet at last burbles largely alone up to its high A flat, and then jumps to a low cadence that finishes just "on the nick" (see Figure 96, b), it is a dull listener who does not glow with some of the gratification that fills the players. Tovey pronounces this scherzo "the most deliciously Viennese of all Brahms's works."

The trio is rather odd: an example of those hobbling syncopations Brahms likes to set for the hands of the pianist to wander over, feeling his way to new keys and harmonies with something of the haphazardness, seemingly, of ice-crystals on a window-pane. The clarinet meanwhile assumes the unfamiliar rôle of bass. In the second half a four-note motive suggestive

Figure 96.

of the first movement crystallizes out, and begins to find its own way to still further agreeably unexpected harmonies. The first tune then returns in full, ending as before with the delighted and delighting gurgles of the clarinet up to its high A flat, and subsidence to the cadence that seems to complete the problem as with a complacent Q.E.D.

The finale, F major and *Vivace,* opens with the striking of of three half-note F's by the piano, forte and carrying accents, that sound like a summons to attention, a promise of important matters to be transacted. Their association with bold eighth-note figuration, the notes detached from each other and well marked, seems further to promise later contrapuntal treatment of the kind in which the composer is so expert. But these promises prove fallacious; although the reiterated half-notes appear frequently through the movement they serve only to give it emphasis rather than any complexity of texture; and in short the mood is here thoroughly care-free and holiday-making, one in which weighty matters are to be avoided. The three insistent half-notes quickly make way, therefore, for a *grazioso* melody for clarinet, half fluent curves and half chuckling staccato notes—and both halves equally good-humored. This is stated, contrasted, and restated with all the leisureliness of a rondo that does not have to find room for much complication. A brief second theme, in which the reiterant half-notes go into the bass (and are sounded also, in diminution, by the clarinet) interrupts the even progress of the stream but a moment; the main theme soon bubbles in again and ripples along to restatement and slight development like a placid river crossing a wide, flat valley.

There are only one or two other diversions in the movement: a brief episode in D minor on a new theme, *piano semplice;* the second theme once more, in the tonic key; an interesting, rather mysterious pause, where the clarinet sounds the repeated half-notes three several times, in as many keys, ending with the hollow low A of its chalumeau. All this is by way of preparation for the final expanse of the main theme, broken up for a moment into *staccato* chords in the piano and *staccato* bass in the clarinet as if its stream had encountered some rocks or a gentle slope in its bed and was dreaming of rapids—but soon settling down again into its placid lowland ripple, with the ocean not far away after all.

CHAPTER XXIV

THE CLARINET SONATA IN E FLAT, OPUS 120, NO. 2

TYPICAL clarinet music is the opening theme (Figure 97, a) of the E flat Sonata. The fluent rises and dips of its first few measures, the wide yet perfectly unagitated jump to the high A flat in measure 5, and the impassive volubility of the curves that follow it up to the cadence, are exactly what the clarinet can do with a supreme felicity. In the two measures (not shown in the illustration) that follow the theme and bridge over to its repetition, are exemplified the extraordinary power of the instrument to utter the maximum number of notes in the minimum interval of time,—and all with amusingly unruffled glibness, complete nonchalance and *sang-froid*. It is like the princess in the fairy story, from whose mouth, every time she opened it, fell quantities of pearls—or were they diamonds? In the case of the clarinet they are pearls—whole strings, garlands, and festoons of them!

The effect of fluent flexibility conveyed on the purely physical plane by this ease of utterance is confirmed and enhanced by the mental freshness, the unexpectedness, with which the motives are manipulated, and by the delightfully neat conciseness of the resulting forms. The repetition of the theme is generated in a highly unforeseen way. We notice in the figure, first, that the chief motive is the turn around and back to E flat of the opening measure; second, that a bolder motive, with jumps, appears in measure 3; and third, that the bass

a. Allegro amabile   *Figure 97.*

moves up the scale, a note to each measure, from the tonic, E flat, to the dominant B flat, about which the last four measures revolve, and on which they finally cadence. When Brahms comes to repeat his theme, he simply, like the imaginative contrapuntist he is, puts the "turn-around" motive in the bass, filling the upper parts with pleasant arpeggios. Then, when he reaches the dominant, he makes the piano play with the bolder motive, fretting it to agitation, lashing it into uneven rhythms of a measure and a half each, until the clarinet breaks in, *forte*, with the "turn-around" motive on high B flat and, relenting, comes down, in four measures more, by a gradual descent—registral, dynamic, rhythmic—to silence and pause, before the second theme.

This theme is not so much a complete contrasting melody, such as we find in the early works, as a continuation, a new groups of crystals, so to speak, precipitated from the same mother-liquor. The upward octave with which it opens is obviously derived from the recent agitations of the piano; but this octave jump at once begins to go its own way—and the way is one that would occur to no one but a confirmed contrapuntist. What happens, as one may see by a glance at Figure 97, b, is that the piano bass, entering on the heels of the clarinet melody, imitates it in *strict canon at the fourth* (or the fifth below, which is the same thing) *after one beat*. This is certainly not one of the easiest types of canon to write; but it is here written with such ease that we might well fail to notice it was a canon at all, and what we do chiefly notice may very likely be that adorable *dolce* of the clarinet, in the fifth measure, which we may suppose to be a purely sensuous effect until we try deducting from it, by making the bass read any other way, the intellectual delight due to the canon.

After the *forte* for piano solo which concludes this theme there seems to be a sort of rudimentary conclusion theme suggested by the clarinet. But it loses itself in sequences, and presently merges into another bit of casual dialogue on the upward octave jump, and a summary citation from the main theme.

The same casualness is carried over from the exposition into the development. This we may roughly divide into four sec-

tions, all concerned in one way or another with the three motives now before us. The first is little more than a resumption
of the version of the first theme, in both its motives, that we
have already heard in its repetition near the start. The second
is more arresting, especially in its odd sonority. While the
piano outlines the second theme, in mild tones, in G minor,
the clarinet sounds its lowest note, D, full of what Tovey calls
the "dramatic blue grotto hollowness and coldness" of its
lowest octave, as a pedal point bass, in a series of sighs. It ut-
ters, or, as the French would say, more vividly than we can,
"pushes" these sighs with an actual physical impact that makes
the passage unforgettably lugubrious.

The third section contains one of Brahms's ingenious extensions of a theme by elaboration of some special feature of it.
In this case the piano sounds the "turning-around" motive, now
made more suspensive than at first by being placed on dominant
rather than tonic harmony, and while it holds the fourth and
last note of the turn the clarinet adds the remaining notes of
the original melodic figure, and multiplies them by repetitions. This is done twice, once in G, once in C, but both
times in quietude. A series of antiphonal plays between the two
instruments then proceeds to invade this quietude and fret it
toward climax, at the top of which comes the fourth and most
striking section of all, where the "turning-around" motive is
multiplied in constantly changing rhythms of the greatest ingenuity by the clarinet and presently set in strange groping
harmonies by the piano (Figure 97, c shows the melody only,
with a slight indication of the eerie piano harmonies). After
this, recapitulation soon follows; and the movement closes with
a short, rather elegiac coda.

As a foil to the graceful, almost feminine character of the
first movement, we find as middle movement a bold and passionate scherzo of an unusual type. It is, to be sure, in the

Figure 98.

familiar form of three-part scherzo with trio and return; but
it is in the severe key of E flat minor, it is marked *Allegro
appassionato*, and its main theme is of heroic vigor, while the
trio is on a melody of unusual nobility, and unusually broadly
treated, even for Brahms. The note of boldness is struck at
once in the theme by its upward leap of a sixth from a firm

anacrusis, and by its strong diatonic continuation (Figure 98, a). In the first period, shown in the illustration, and uttered *forte* by the clarinet over sonorous piano arpeggios, this upward leap occurs three times; and the period is immediately repeated by piano, solo. A contrast made from the cadence leads quickly back; but at the return we already see that treatment is to be as

Figure 99.

* * *The melody passes from right hand to left.*

bold as theme, for the anacrusis and leap in the piano are not followed by the rest of the melody, but by an answer from the clarinet (Figure 98, b) with extension of the upper note so long that the original six-note motive becomes a full four-measure phrase. This is repeated, with strongly modelled harmonies; and only after that and a further pair of measures in the original rhythm does the theme in its pristine state recur. Thus warned how free the treatment is to be, we are not surprised at a considerable passage in which the group of four eighth-notes in downward scale is isolated and developed, —by clarinet, by piano, by both together. Nobly conceived is the peroration, an augmentation of the opening measures, so placed rhythmically (see the eighth measure of Figure 99) that the anacrusis occupies a whole (light) measure, and the eighth-notes become quarters. The result is a magnificent, deliberate phrase of no less than fourteen measures (with one preceding one of anacrusis) carrying itself with regal splendor from the upward jump of a sixth to the nobly-poised downward fifth of its cadence on the low E flat of the clarinet.

In all the chamber music there is no more beautiful use of variations than in the last movement of this sonata, essentially a theme, five variations, and a free coda derived from the same theme. Simple as it sounds, this theme, arranged for piano in Figure 100, is a marvelously subtle piece of composition—of course much of its subtlety lies precisely in that final simplicity of effect. Here is its ground plan:

Phrase 1 (Statement) 4 measures, cadence in B flat, the dominant key.

Phrase 2 (Confirmation) 4 measures, same cadence.

Phrase 3 (Contrast) 2 measures, cadence in the mediant, G minor.

Phrase 4 (Return) 4 measures, full cadence, E flat.

Figure 100.

In all four of the variations in major, the listener will find
helpful landmarks in the retention of the relative lengths of
phrases: 4, 4, 2, 4, and of cadences: B flat, B flat, G minor,
E flat. In the fifth variation, where the mode changes to minor,
and the tempo accelerates to *Allegro*, the phrase lengths still

retain their relative though not their absolute value, becoming 8, 8, 4, 8; while the cadences are B flat, B flat, G flat (in place of G minor), E flat.

In other respects the variations are strikingly different. The first is one of those highly imaginative variations, made by simplification rather than by complication, which have all the suggestiveness of Chinese poetry. Its texture recalls the severe and pure contrapuntal lines of the posthumous Chorale Preludes. In the second phrase the rhythm reduces to plain eighths, but in the others there is somewhat more subordinate rhythm. In the last phrase the subdominant, A flat, from the theme is amplified by its own subdominant, D flat, a natural emphasis on this dark coloring.

Variation II is piquant, almost pert, with its coy jumps in the melody and its voluble triplet sixteenth-note arpeggios accompanying.

In Variation III, though the triplet groups are changed to even smaller values (thirty-seconds), the curves are now so graceful and sinuous, and there is such exquisite give-and-take between the instruments, that the effect is less of speed than of leisurely unfoldment of a lovely design. This is a sort of mosaic work in which the stones are living melodies.

In Variation IV we have an even more far-reaching simplification of the theme than in I, and hence an even more suggestive one. Almost everything is left to our memories and imaginations; of the theme little more than the harmonic basis remains, with an occasional hint of a motive. The rhythm is furthermore so simplified that the melody, given in the first and third phrases to the piano, in the others to both instruments in counterpoint, moves only by eighths, against which the bass has even more stately and mysterious quarters, so placed as to cross the normal accents and thus almost imperceptibly obscure or trouble the meter. Finally, in the phrases where only the piano has the melody—or what little melody there is —this bass is made even more strange by being sighed out by the clarinet in its hollowest chalumeau notes. . . . The whole variation is of an unforgettable eerie elusiveness.

After this moment of audible hush, as it were, we plunge into a final variation of full energy, *Allegro*, E flat minor (the mode adds to the sense of stormy impetuosity), *forte ben marcato*. There is here a new momentum, a strange forward urge, that presages the approaching end. With the change back to major there is a momentary quietening, as the cadence theme with its repeated notes comes in for a brief tranquil development as coda. It is but momentary. If the evening shadows seem about to gather they are promptly dissipated; the opening motive reappears in a new rhythmic variant, condensed to headlong impulsiveness; and with all manner of cross accents and energetic diminutions of various parts of the theme the end is reached in highest exuberance of good spirits, and in the full noontide of E flat major daylight.

CONCLUSION

In our study of the twenty-four chamber music works of Brahms we have purposely adopted an analytic, technical, impersonal mode of attack. Our effort has been to see what the works are in themselves, as musical constructions, and only secondarily to interpret them as expressions of a personality, since that aspect of them is finally less important than their pure beauty. So studying, we have observed an almost constant growth from the turgidity and confusion of the early version of the Trio, opus 8, through the vigorous but somewhat extravagant and ununified vitality of the early piano Quartets and Quintet, to the full, controlled beauty of the string Quartets, then to the mellow loveliness of the G major Violin Sonata and the mature power of the Viola Quintet in G major, and finally to the sad but clear autumnal beauty of the Clarinet Quintet. It may be of interest now in concluding our study to check these impersonal qualities by glancing for a moment more directly at the person behind them.

In all his works, whether turgid in youth, powerfully moulded in maturity, or a little stoical and severe in old age, Brahms is essentially simple, strong, universal. There is in him not a trace of the exotic or the esoteric. His melody has the diatonic ruggedness of German folk-song; chromatic elements are rare and incidental. His harmony is based on tonic, dominant, subdominant, as frankly as Beethoven's, though with half-lights and with uses of subtle tonal relations that make it his own. His rhythm builds the fundamental duple and triple measures that are common property into the most masterly many-sided structures that have ever been imagined in music. Here he is a supreme master. Thus in all the elements of music he shews himself a *central* person, a person interested in what is universally human rather than in any eccentricities. We find this impression corroborated by what we know of him as a man: by his love of children and of humble people, by his dislike and avoidance of snobs, flatterers, and sycophants of all varieties. One recalls the anecdote of the celebrity-hunter whom he sent over the hills in a fruitless search for "my brother, the composer." One remembers his loathing for the discussion of music, for "art" talk and sentimental babble. Arthur M. Abel has told how he was snubbed by him, at a first meeting, for unwisely trying to praise his music. At a second meeting, better inspired, he started talking about the Bible, and Brahms joined in with enthusiasm.

Much of the extraordinary technical, intellectual, and emotional deepening we have traced from the opus 8 Trio to the two great quintets was due, of course, to the tireless studies he was always making of the music of others. His library, inherited by the *Gesellschaft der Musikfreunde*, witnesses the wide range of his interests; notes preserved at the *Brahms Haus* in Gmunden cover the works of composers of many nations and periods; and his letters touch on all manner of scores with keenest interest and most penetrating understanding. Spitta has remarked his use of the old modes, of complex rhythms long fallen into disuse, of augmentation, diminution, and other contrapuntal devices of earlier centuries, of the *basso ostinato*, the passacaglia, and the chaconne; and comments truly: "His passion for learning wandered into every field, and resulted in a rich and most original culture of mind." He was in short refreshingly free from the fear of influences we find in weak, ill-nourished minds; his appetite for good music was insatiable, and the question of who happened to write it did not trouble one so happily modest, so free from vanity. "What Brahms is among the composers" said a speaker at a supper, "this Rauenthaler is among the wines." "Take it away, then," said Brahms, "and bring us a bottle of Bach."

Brahms's music is by no means faultless, it is far from perfect—it is too human for that. Its faults, like those of his character, are on the surface, patent for all to see. Thirty years ago, when his music was beginning to make its way in this country, it was always being accused of "dryness," of "over-intellectuality." Of course this is always the charge of those who resent the effort of thought against those who make them think; but there is nevertheless, as we have seen, this much truth in it, that when inspiration momentarily fails, so skillful a technique as Brahms's is likely to go on by habit, and to produce routine. Nowadays however the favorite charge against him is precisely the opposite one, of over-ripeness, of romanticism, even of sentimentality. Undoubtedly Brahms is strongly romantic, though he is seldom if ever sentimental. Probably the answer to this criticism is that, if he is sometimes too romantic, fashion is at present far too anti-romantic; some sort of balance will no doubt in the long run be struck.

Just as the quality in Brahms's music we most constantly return to with a supreme joy is its universality, its nobility, its strong and manly beauty, so the final virtue of his character is its self-reliance, masculine strength, quiet dignity and reticence. During the whole period of his life the tendencies he embodies were out of fashion, and in many quarters he was neglected, misrepresented, or misunderstood. The "new music" of Liszt, Wagner's "music of the future," Berlioz's picture and program music were in the ascendant, and Brahms was looked upon by many, as Bach had been before him, as an outdated reactionary. Save for one ill-considered open letter, published in his youth, he paid no overt attention to these mis-representations. He went silently about his business, writing symphonies without picturesque titles, studying structure more than color, accepting stoically his failures with the public (though he could not accept them for a wife, and therefore denied himself marriage). His replies to his detractors were not in words but in works, of which we have just tasted the living beauties of twenty-four in that department of chamber music in which, because of its emphasis on plastic beauty, its invitation to thought and feeling, its inhospitality to sensationalism, he was peculiarly at home. He met the world with a reticence that equalled its curiosity, with an irony subtle enough to protect the softest of hearts, the most poetic of minds. "What I am," says Thoreau, "I am, and say not. Being is the great explainer." If ever a musician could truly say that, it was Brahms. . . .

He is gone, but his works remain.

INDEX

NOTE. The references to individual works of Brahms will be found under the headings, Trio, Quartet, Quintet, Sextet, Sonata, etc., followed by mention of instruments and key; the chapter devoted to the work in question is indicated by italics, passing references by ordinary type; f., or ff., following a page-number, indicate that the following page or pages continue discussing the same subject. Example: "Quartet, C minor, vii, viii, *87–96, 97*ff., 117, 177, 267."

A

Abel, Arthur M., 268.

Aichholz, Miller zu, vii.

America, first performance of Brahms chamber music in, 3–4.

America, Musical (magazine), ix.

Anacrustic rhythms, give variety in second version of B major Trio, 8; happy use of in B flat Sextet, 14; exciting effect of, 20; used in climax, 28; in scherzo of Piano Quintet, 50f.; opposed to thetic in E minor Cello Sonata, 69; in minuet of Cello Sonata, 72; in variation-theme of B flat Quartet, 125; displacing "empty firsts," 131; contrasted with thetic, 142; in the fugue of the F major Viola Quintet, 157ff.; caressing, 171; syncopated, 182; in the *Poco Allegretto* of the G major Viola Quintet, 211f.; in the Clarinet Quintet, 233; intensified by lengthening of anacrusis, 234; sadness of, 237; anacrusis becoming a whole measure, 262.

Augmentation, 47, 59, 125, 139, 142, 147, 157, 162f., 164, 179, 185, 197, 237, 241, 249, 250. *See also* Rhythm, elongations of.

B

Bach, J. S., 19, 32, 142, 210, 223, 269.

Balfe, M. W., 225.

Bass as part of theme, 171, 189.

Beckerath, W. von, drawing of Brahms at the piano by, 25.

Beethoven, Ludwig van, 5, 14, 19, 22, 25, 30, 32, 61, 89, 108, 155, 223, 251, 267.

Bergmann, Carl, 3.

Berlioz, Hector, 269.

Betti, Adolfo, ix, 88, 117.

Billroth, Theodor, 111, 219.

Brahms, Johannes, manuscripts of, vii; *Brahms Haus* in Gmunden, vii, 204, 268; piano arrangements of works of, viii; complete works of, issued by Breitkopf and Härtel, viii; thematic catalogue of works, viii; rhythm, mastery of, ix, 7, *see also* Pace, Meter, Rhythm; born Hamburg, May 7, 1833, 4; musical adolescence, 13; "The Brahms Leit-motive," 34, 71, *see also* "Frei aber froh"; retort to a charge of plagiarism, 169; "C minor mood," 177; failure of health and death, 219; mannerisms of style, 221, 223, 227, 253; personality, 267–270; simplicity, 267; scholarship, 268; modesty, 269; lapses into routine, 269; manly strength and reticence, 269–270.

C

Cadence, the natural place for "preparation," 16; banal, 30; feminine, 52, 245; made from thematic motive, 72; Straussian, 109; Mozart makes a phrase-opening from one, 118; Brahms makes one from an opening, 121; sudden evasion in, 125; witty abridgment of, 125; contrasts in strength of, 136; richly simple, 153, 155; weightiness of Neapolitan sixth in, 244; generated from another theme, 245; cadences as landmarks in a theme, 264. *See also* Tonic-dominant relation.

and triple ingeniously combined, 183ff.; restlessness in, a symptom of defective control, 225f.; caressing triple, 239; notating same music in different meters, 242. *See also* Pace, Pulse, Rhythm.

Morbidezza, in certain late themes of Brahms, 225, 253.

Motivation, contrasting, in C minor Quartet, 89f.; in coda of G major Viola Quintet, 209.

Motive transformation, 26, 137f., 164, 178f.

Motives, putting the same in different parts of the phrase, 199.

Mozart, W. A., 14, 22, 24, 32, 70, 89, 118, 121, 155.

Mühlfeld, Richard, 202, 220, 241, 247.

N

"Nachklang," 134.

Neapolitan sixth, 153, 244.

Niemann, Walter, *Brahms,* English translation, viii, 220.

Nikisch, Arthur, 247.

O

Oberlaender, Gustav, vii.

Overstreet, Harry A., *Influencing Human Behavior,* 117ff.

P

Pace, irregularity of, does not cure monotony of rhythm, 7ff.; unifies contrasting rhythms, 14, 49; changing its relation to rhythmic groups, 34; why Brahms's music needs a deliberate, 204. *See also* Pulse, Meter, Rhythm.

Pedal-points, 47, 71, 152, 191–194.

Pedal sustainment, the string quartet lacks, 100.

Perpetuum mobile, 156.

Phrases, three measure and other unusual lengths, 74; echoed and extended, 169f.; changing positions of motives within, 199, 201.

Phraseology, flexibility in, 170f.

Piano arrangements, viii.

Piano Concerto in D minor, 87f., 109; in B flat, 80.

Piano Sonata in F minor, 110.

Piano, rhythmic incisiveness of, 43; fusion with other instruments, 70ff.

"Plagiarism," Brahms's indifference to textual resemblances, 169.

Polytonality, 155.

"Portmanteau movements" (made up of sections in contrasting but related tempi), 104, 153, 174, 242.

Prater Park, Vienna, 206ff. *See also* Vienna.

"Preparations," 9, 16, 20, 45f., 48, 59f., 85, 93, 133, 151, 166, 236.

Prize-song, Wagner's, 169ff.

Prolixity in early works, 23ff., 34, 43ff., 54f. *See* Concentration of later style.

Pulse, Brahms's use of, seldom primitive, 31, 49. *See also* Pace.

Q

Quartet, C minor, vii, viii, *87–96,* 97ff., 117, 177, 267.

Quartet, A minor, viii, 87, *97–107,* 117, 123, 267.

Quartet, B flat, viii, 19, 87, *117–126,* 243, 267.

Quartet, Piano, G minor, vii, viii, *22–32,* 34, 49, 87f., 103, 108, 112, 140, 241, 267.

Quartet, Piano, A, vii, viii, 22, *33–42,* 44, 87, 112, 227, 267.

Quartet, Piano, C minor, 87, *108–116,* 177.

Quintet, Piano and String Quartet, viii, 22, *43–54,* 58, 87f., 109, 112, 267.

Quintet, Viola and String Quartet, F, viii, 87, *149–159,* 211.

Quintet, Viola and String Quartet, G, vii, viii, 103, 189, *202–218,* 219, 221, 267.

Quintet, Clarinet and String Quartet, vii, viii, 19, 88, 189, 202, 219, 221, 230, *231–247,* 267.

R

"Rain theme," ("Regenlied"), 134ff.

Repetition, modified, 17, 19, 74.

Revision, exemplified in B major Trio, 4; three forms of Piano Quintet, 43; deliberateness in, 87; recasting works for different instruments, 88; works illustrating long-continued, 109; cannot always succeed, 116.

Rhythm, anacrustic, *see* Anacrustic rhythms; Brahmsian "hobbling," 68, 173, 190, 253; elongations of, 42, 132, 142, 163, *see also* Augmentation; "empty first beats" in, *see* "Empty first beats"; feminine, 52, 212; intentional ambiguity of, 184; monotony of, in first works, 7, in last works, 223, 225; shifted, 59,